Lifestyle Management

An Ever-Changing and Evolving Process

Jeremiah Gagnon

ISBN 978-1-64299-885-6 (paperback)
ISBN 978-1-64299-886-3 (digital)

Copyright © 2018 by Jeremiah Gagnon

All rights reserved. No part of this publication may be reproduced, distributed, or transmitted in any form or by any means, including photocopying, recording, or other electronic or mechanical methods without the prior written permission of the publisher. For permission requests, solicit the publisher via the address below.

Christian Faith Publishing, Inc.
832 Park Avenue
Meadville, PA 16335
www.christianfaithpublishing.com

Printed in the United States of America

Acknowledgement(s)

Thanks to our Lord God, family and contacts throughout my life, for they have given me first hand exposure and experiences. It has been experiences of life that presented me with the information that helps us see ourselves more completely.

Thanks to my wife, for her straight forwardness, my daughters Maureen, Gemarie and son Emerson, for teaching me how to love more perfectly. (Especially during their teenage years.) And thanks to Gemarie, for her excitement and encouragement to get this book finished. To Emerson, for his thoroughness and meticulous proper mastery of rhetoric.

Contents

Introduction 7
1. Balance 9
2. Creating Balance 13
3. What Do I Do? What Can I Do? 18
4. Realms of Activity 22
5. Breaking Down Activity 27
6. Limiting Factors 59
7. Balanced Lifestyle Survey 72
8. Why We Do the Things We Do? 83
9. Components of Self 96
10. Socialization 113
11. Desocialization 131
12. Communication 148

Conclusion 157
Glossary 159
Self Exploratory Exercises 161
Balanced Lifestyle Survey 162
Group Benefit Exercise! 166

Introduction

Throughout my professional career and life, I have been fascinated with the fact that there are so many things to do, so many activities to choose from!

As far back as I can remember, from the youngest age, I wondered about activity and why one does certain things. Of course, this was probably brought on by being asked the eternal question. The question we all are asked at one time or another, usually after we have done something way out of the ordinary and/or realm of acceptability in someone else's eye. That question(s) being, "Why did you do that?" "Why on Earth did you do that?" or "What on Earth got into you?" Take your pick! It was usually followed by "You idiot" or "What were you *thinking*?"

After having heard the question often enough and observing many other activity choices, one begins to wonder themselves, *Why did I do that? With so many activities to choose, why on earth did I choose that one?* Knowing in advance, full well, and with very little reasoning required, the chance of a good outcome is limited at the very best. Unaware at the time that this would become a lifelong quest! A quest to learn and understand why people actually do the things they do.

The motive, or should I say the motivation, became a fascination. I never believed, even as a young child, that there are no random acts. All activity is purposeful, some beneficial to oneself and some not so beneficial to oneself or others. Some activities and actions inspire, some destroy. Some done consciously, some done unconsciously. As we start to understand the vastness of this subject, you, too, will begin to understand and have some insight as to why we make the choices we make. I devoted my life and career to this understanding.

INTRODUCTION

The purpose of this book is to share what I have been enlightened to. The sharing with any and all who wish to understand themselves and their choice of involvement, and to learn to manage their life more effectively. Throughout my professional career, many colleagues, coworkers, and recipients of my service have suggested that I write, copy, copyright, and publish this information—the information that I compiled and presented many times throughout the years of my practice.

I have shared this and other related material many times in educational settings, in-service trainings, and conferences throughout the United States.

I always believed I own nothing when it comes to the knowledge and material used to assess and educate clients, patients, colleagues, coworkers, students, and fellow professionals. All I have, has been given to me by those whom I have learned from, studied from, and served. Through exploration, research, comparing statistics, etc., I have gained insight. So nothing truly belongs to me and I am willing to share all I know in hopes it will assist all to make more productive choices in living their lives as productively and as enjoyably as possible.

Chapter 1

Balance

Where on earth does one begin? When exploring the history and the evolution of activity, let us look at the beginning, as we know it.

At the dawn of creation, we have in the book of Genesis, been given a brief insight into the activity of Adam and Eve. What is apparent, that life and existence was paradise. No need for toil, just be! To touch, taste, and exist in a harmonious state with the environment. Life, from what we know from the written word in a glimpse, was a life of leisure. Adam and Eve were to eat (except for one thing, of course), sleep, enjoy the other creatures, the fruit of the land and of course, each other.

With free rein, how does one find balance? How does one even come to an understanding of it in one's life when there seems to be no limits? How does one find peace? How does one come to an understanding that there is an impact on us, others, and all living things by the actions we take?

The key to all of life and survival is achieving a balance.

What does this mean?

It is different for every living thing, every plant, every animal, ecosystem, and/or environment. Without balance, our environment cannot survive nor the creatures within it. Although life always seeks balance and some will create their own in the harshest of conditions and areas of our planet.

BALANCE

Can we live without balance?

So many of us do, but for how long and how healthfully and *productively* is the question. (I will use the term *productively* throughout this book to describe the level of health, enjoyment, and satisfaction of our personal existence.) This is the real question and answers we all wish to find out!

Many an industry has been developed over the millennium to satisfy our quest for balance, happiness, enjoyment, and pleasure. All promise to make life easier so we can have more time to pursue an even greater productive level of balance in our lives.

With the world so vast and complex as it is with so many unique ecosystems and so many unique species of life in so many different environments, where does one begin to seek balance for oneself?

Throughout this book, we will be referencing one species: homo-sapiens; that of man. Other than coming in various sizes, shapes, and colors, it is a homogeneous bunch. This is the life form we share and must live within. Not to mention, the only one I can say I have experienced, being one of the same species, wearing its shoes, following its path, and studying it. I have never been anything else, and I don't suspect to ever be anything else until I meet my maker.

With that said, let us begin our journey. The journey to a greater understanding of ourselves and what our needs may be to achieve this thing we call balance. To do so, we must first understand what balance is.

The term itself encompasses vast meaning. Basically, the meaning of balance is an equilibrium; equality of various elements; the equality in amounts; stability; and what I like most about the definition is "a pleasing harmony of various elements, a harmonious proposition." Isn't that a great thought and wouldn't that be a great state of being and existence?

It is a fairly simple thing for one to understand certain principles and components of oneself. It is another thing to achieve a productive balance between the components of self. I will refer to this as the *balanced point*, the elements of which we will explore in great detail later. In addition, it's another thing still to maintain the balanced point for it is never a static state of being.

LIFESTYLE MANAGEMENT

We will always need to compensate for changes in life. We must adjust to the basic and typical life changes, such as growth, age, illness, accident, relationships, careers, and environments. These everyday challenges of life we can expect, and will experience as we live and work, all of which will require adjustments.

The further we go into this opening chapter the more perplexed and complicated it may seem to achieve balance in one's life. Our quest, along with reaching it and means of maintaining it once we reach a harmonious existence and comfort level within our self and lifestyle, is to keep it.

It is easy to get that perception when we start to see all the things there are to consider, due to all of the interesting and vast array of variables and interferences that affect each of us. We are faced with many things that will affect our physical, emotional, intellectual, and social states of being on any given day.

Let's look at the potential interference, or simply, changes that occur throughout typical days in our lives. We will also review changes that can and do occur during various phases of our lives which we grow and evolve through. Each brings a unique set of issues that interfere with our choices and decision-making.

We all love change, right? We like it when it's good; not so much when it's not so good. The fact is, the only thing in life we can count on and is consistent is change. Whether we like it or not, it is inevitable. Each year we change as we grow, learn, and experience life. The seasons change, each offer its own beauty, harshness, conditions and opportunities, as does each phase/stage of life. When or should I say, if we adjust accordingly, we thrive. Each day brings different weather conditions, new challenges, and new potential for any number of planned and unplanned events. As each of us get out of bed and begin to roam the house, go to work, school, live, and move in our world, we will experience changes. Even as we are driving down the street, changes can occur without any prewarning.

To establish and achieve balance, we must constantly make up for the many things that offset it, due to things that may occur from no fault of our own. Let us keep steady the scale, so to speak. This is a good image to keep in mind. Libra holding the scale—the symbol of

BALANCE

balance. Each of us holds the scale. It is part of our internal makeup, seeking and achieving the equilibrium of balance within ourselves for our own lives. The tools are built into our design.

When I contemplate balance, I see the word in my mind's eye. I see a vision of scales, a balance beam, and a tight rope. While holding true to my mission in life, I set my mind to the exploration of those activities themselves. Let's examine the similarities of each activity just mentioned—the scales, seesaw, or as some refer to it, a teeter-totter, balance beam, and tight rope. These activities present an image of requiring an extreme focus. Also, with each of these is the need of extraordinary gifted physical coordination and body control—the very skills required for them to be performed.

Imagine if the superb control, concentration, steadiness, and musculature required for these activities do not automatically adjust to the other forces that play against it. The one performing it falls off the wire. The seesaw may stay in a down position on the heavier side; it is stuck. The balance beam is not stabilized and wobbles. The scales are tipped, never to be equalized. Hopefully, no one will injure themselves in performing one of those activities. (If they do, they or someone else may be asking, "Why did I do that?"). If an incident occurs as they will, one can get right back on the equipment after making appropriate adjustments and resume the routine. Just as with each one of us, many factors can and will tip the scale of balance. The balance, which in some cases, we have worked hard to establish. The goal for each of my readers, is to gain the knowledge needed to reset the scales. To learn more about themselves and gather the information you need, which lies within each of us. So we can resume our mission as we move and evolve through life.

In the world of acrobatics, there is one assigned as the balancer who is the base, the foundation, or the footer, so to speak. His job is to stabilize the others in the act, performing towers or sculptors of humanity. When it comes to our life, we are the balancer or the stabilizer. We are and must be the solid base. We must come to understand ourselves so we can make the decisions necessary that will help each of us to achieve and maintain productive balance in our own lives throughout our lives.

So let us begin this journey in search of self!

Chapter 2

Creating Balance

We all innately know and understand the balance of life. At least, in its most basic necessities.

An example of this is a mother and her firstborn child. She makes sure her newborn is nourished, warm, and rested. When the needs of the infant are met in a timely manner, then balance for its healthy little life is achieved.

Simply, it has no other needs. Initially, of course, it is dependent. The infant instinctively knows how to let those around it, of whom it is dependent on, know when it needs something to keep its little life in balance. It isn't born with attached instructions for itself or its new mother. The child, as well as the mother, understands its needs. Of course, this loving, lovable little bundle of joy creates a huge imbalance in the life of others.

It is the wise who will anticipate and prepare *physically, emotionally, intellectually, and socially* for the changes. Arranging for the readjusting of the scale *to assure the* maintenance of a healthy and productive balance of one's life during this major change, will make a world of difference for all involved. What is that old proverb, "An ounce of prevention, is worth a pound of cure?" So true!

Remember the comment earlier—*interference*—and I say that with a great smile on my face, especially with this example. A newborn is a wonderful interference in our life and more than likely our lifestyle. We will devote an entire chapter to each of life's involvement areas. These involvement areas are key components/areas of activity to help identify balance or imbalances in our life. Once we have that information we can make appropriate adjustments when wonderful or disastrous interferences present themselves into our world. We will explore basic behaviors and social needs that we all must gratify effectively if we are going to exist and hopefully thrive in this God-given opportunity we call life. All living things need to find, create, establish, and maintain balance in order to exist.

We have heard it for years the need to have balanced levels of sleep, balanced diet and nutrition, balance in the workplace, balanced exercise (muscle confusion techniques now available in routines keep our physical body in balance and not overusing certain muscles or muscle groups), balanced levels of light and darkness, and it goes on and on. Let's not forget balancing of your budget!

Balancing your time with all these items just mentioned can be confusing and overwhelming if we don't understand the basics. This book is dedicated to understanding what these basic components of self are.

It's easy to see just by looking at the simplified comparisons of things we need to consider when attempting to achieve the balanced point, how things can go south quickly. Or as my father used to say, "Go to hell in a hand basket" really quick if we don't balance these items in a reasonable amount of time.

I mentioned briefly in the introduction that many an industry and agency have been developed to capitalize on helping us achieve balance in life. The FDA for one, (an important one for sure), is focusing on the safety of the food and drug components of health and nutrition. I, for one, get way more food and nutrition than what my body needs to maintain a balanced nutritional level. Drugs—I won't say much about that, other than I am not a strong component of dietary supplements nor am I a component for the treating of symptoms of the mind and body through chemical introduction to our system. Especially, if the body may produce it naturally or extract what we need from our food intake when it is functioning effectively and we maintain a healthy diet.

LIFESTYLE MANAGEMENT

Yes, in many cases and circumstances, medications and supplements may be necessary and are a required component of our overall health and well-being. A good example is the need for insulin when the body stops producing it. The chemical imbalances created by our body or brain malfunctions may require the use of medications and may be absolutely necessary if directed and supervised under medical supervision.

I am a strong advocate of natural methods wherever possible. I'll share personal experiences with anyone willing to listen of things that have worked and work for me. But, each of us is different and unique as to our needs and what works best for us. There is not one simple recipe that works for all. We are all separate and unique individuals/creatures. The next few chapters will give your insight into what you will need to help make the best decisions for you.

The brain is such a remarkable thing, as is the body. Being in the health profession my entire career, I worked in a variety of hospital settings, including drug and alcohol treatment, psychiatric and physical rehabilitation, crisis units, and pain management facilities, as well as in athletic and sports environments. The work throughout my career brought me in contact with people of ages ranging from infants, teens, adults, and geriatric individuals.

I have seen and heard amazing things about the mind and body's potential. We can do remarkable and unbelievable things in recovery, performance, and in emergency situations. I recall attending a neurological conference many years ago, and the keynote speaker was a renowned neurosurgeon who was held in high esteem by his colleagues. He was describing the brain as its own pharmaceutical lab with its ability to produce forms of chemicals that the body needs to maintain balance within itself. It was fascinating! I can still recall to this day, the excitement I had about attending the conference, knowing what I knew about the brain and its functions and wanting to learn more. One of the speaker's initial statements was, "We know nothing about the brain", which was in reference to its potential and our very limited understanding of it at the time. Here I am in the audience. After hearing that, I was thinking to myself, *Great! Just great. That's just great.* Here is the greatest mind on the brain, and he says he knows nothing about the brain. That must mean I know less than nothing.

I'm feeling worse off now about my limited knowledge of the brain than I did before attending the conference.

We know which parts of the brain produce certain things, what parts of the body, and its functions the brain controls.

We are just beginning to understand that the involvement in certain activities can produce certain chemicals in the brain. We have known the effects of extreme physical involvement and the production of endorphins that produce a euphoric sense. We all have heard it before, *the runners' high*, *the zone*, more recently referred to as *it* (He's *it*. She's in *it*). Whatever *it* is when they have *it*, everything clicks.

Due to all the money involved in the athletic and performance enhancement industry, much research and study has been done. This lead to the understanding of endorphins - this morphine type substance that is produced in the brain when one is involved in extreme strenuous activity. Who knows what the science of sport and the human performance science industry will discover next. The brain's natural ability to produce the stimulus needed to perform a certain task or prolong activity is important to survival. We are seeing improvement in one's ability to do certain things. Whether or not the enhanced improvements are produced by training or the introduction of artificial substances to enhance performance is the question.

Who knows what artificial substances may be developed to enhance performance in the future or the effects it may have on the individuals and society. That is another topic we will not go into with this book.

I know every action has a reaction. I believe one day we can get to the point where we understand the brain and its pharmaceutical qualities, and what activities and or thoughts will produce what substances. When we can get to that level of knowledge, then we will be able to develop a strategy to determine which activity will create the exact mix of chemicals needed for each of us to achieve the balanced point. Then, we need to be able to determine at what level of participation and or intensity is necessary to achieve it. Once we have reached that point we won't have to introduce foreign substances into our body. The body itself can and will be able to produce what is necessary naturally once we understand the correct processes. Then, the medical professional, activity specialist, or as my profession identifies, Certified Therapeutic Recreation Specialist (CTRS) could prescribe what activities one could do to create the necessary chemical balance needed within our being. Which will bring us one step closer to a more exact science of how one can manage their life and health more productively.

I will leave that to the researchers and the scientists. I challenge all the health professionals now and of the next generation to do further exploration. I believe, as each generation passes, they are going to need this information more than ever since this society and generation are looking more to an artificial, virtual and sedentary world for its activity, interest, entertainment and other life experiences *instead of the real world.*

Let's get real everyone!

Chapter 3

What Do I Do? What Can I Do?

I have been asked many questions about one's involvement. The two most frequently asked throughout my career as a Lifestyle Management Specialist are these listed below:

"What can I do?"

"What will work for me?"

My response to these are always: "I don't know!", or "Let *us* find out!" My next statement is "Let us find out what we can about you."

My general answer to anyone asking me this question, *"What can I do?"* after accidents or injuries causing loss of limb or illnesses causing lost bodily functions especially in this day and age is, "literally anything you wish".

Many of the inhibitors of the past do not exist today. For example, distance from specific activities we may need to do. We have so many options for travel and transportation. We can be anywhere on earth in a matter of hours. To do whatever we wish to do, covering distance isn't much of an issue as it once was. With automobiles, bus, trains, planes, etc., the only limiting factor here may be the cost.

There is also the fact we are not restricted how a specific activity can be performed as we once may have been in the past. Today, any activity can be modified due to humanity and legislative actions. With the advancements in technology, adaptive equipment, and training techniques, we can make almost any activity possible to do. There isn't much we cannot do in this day and age if the will and desire wells within us. The real question is, are we willing to do what we know may work well for us to achieve balance and experience the gratification in our lives?

This, too, we will discuss later in great detail in following chapters when we are exploring limiting factors that prevent us from getting beyond where we are at any particular stage of our life. If we will not, I call this *our stuck state!* This is when the individual is choosing not to do what is necessary to compensate for limiting factors present in their life at any given time.

Another frequently asked question is *"What can I do, to make my life more meaningful?"*

My response is, again, "Let's find out."

My answer to all these questions as well as all the great mysteries leading us into a productive and gratifying lifestyle is, all our own best answers lie within each one of us! You see, there is no great mystery in creating balance in one's life through the involvement in various activity. The key is understanding who we are and what we bring to the table in life. Also, once we know what our preference and style domains may be, we will explore this in the coming chapters. Then we can begin the process of aligning our involvement in areas we know will be successful for us.

Secondly, we need to make the cognitive commitment to overcome our natural tendencies, which will always interfere and sabotage our efforts when we strive to create the balance, needed to get what we so greatly desire—that being a state of wellness and well-being. We all have options and resources to meet our personal needs. Unless, of course, there are extenuating circumstances which are very rare.

I have collected filing cabinet upon filing cabinet of materials I have gathered throughout my career of all sorts of resources and activities from all over the world. My thought process leading to this collection was I would have the needed information when being asked these common questions. I could simply go to my files and find precisely what will work for this individual, patient, or client, and get them back on track right now. I could say, "Here you go," then prescribe thirty minutes a day, three times per week—simple and done. Next, appointment please!

I would have made a fortune!

I actually think some of the physicians I worked with over the years may have thought that may have been what I did. They may have had difficult patient(s) who may not have done well or responded well to treatment. When nothing else worked, they would say "Let's send them to Jeremiah." Next thing you know, they are doing a little better and are a little more receptive to the other treatments being offered in the hospital, unit, or therapeutic setting.

As I mentioned, each individual is unique. Each have different interests, likes, dislikes, needs, backgrounds and experiences. Each have different gifts, goals, and functional capabilities, not to mention age, disability, social, emotional, physical, intelligence, and cognitive development. There is no cookie-cutter approach that will work for everyone. All activity, except those of thought and biological/body functions, has components necessary for involvement outside of us, yet all the answers to what works for us are inside. We must explore each—the external and internal. Believe me, the vastness of each is great and can be mind-boggling!

In this book, I will attempt to assist each of you to find the uniqueness within and about you. Yes, there are a fair handful of things we need to know and understand about ourselves before we will make the appropriate life-enriching decisions and commitment to effectively manage our life to achieve a healthy balance. Yes, balance when there may not appear to be any possibility due to normal rigors of our daily activity schedules (work, chore, and play).

If you go through this process outlined in this book, you are going to learn more about yourself than you ever cared to. You will have the information needed to make appropriate and productive decisions that will assist in keeping your life in balance and on an even keel. The contents, at the very least, give the reader a knowledge base on how to counteract imbalances before they set in and disrupt or devastate our well-being.

LIFESTYLE MANAGEMENT

Devastating effects can and do come in many ways, such as the feeling of wasting our time, listlessness, restlessness, emptiness, limited sense of self value, loneliness, anxiety, and depression. I can literally go on indefinitely, describing symptomatology that many of my patients and clients have described to me over the years.

Chapter 4

Realms of Activity

There are so many activities to choose from. It soon became apparent, I was using up too much space with my filing cabinets, and yet was still just barely scratching the surface in the numbers of activity available and the possibilities of options we all have.

Activity is defined as normal function of body and mind. Okay, so that very simply states, anything and everything can be an activity. We look to and refer to this word generally as something to do or be done. Let us explore or attempt to narrow the vastness of activity, since the number of activity possibilities are endless. When attempting to manage our lives as productively as we can, it is necessary to be selective with the activity(s) we chose to do and when. Also how much time can we spend or will we spend to do the things needed to be done to achieve the balance we need? With endless options, limited time and only one life span, where and how do we start?

I have found it easiest to break down activity into three different divisions. It is important to distinguish and to divide each, before we can begin the journey and take the first steps to manage our life. If we do not divide and keep separate, we will not experience the full, maximum potential and quality each activity division brings to our life.

These three divisions of activity are *work, chore,* and *play*. We will explore each and what it entails. If we look at activity and divide it in this manner, we immediately see the distinct difference, as well

LIFESTYLE MANAGEMENT

as the importance of each individual part. We will begin by explaining each division, along with why each part is so beneficial in the maintaining of proper balance between each division.

Work. This word has one of the largest definitions in Webster's seventh collegiate edition of the dictionary. The definition is physical or mental effort, job, occupation, profession, labor, doing or acting upon, undertaking, to utilize, prepare oneself, cause to function, to make one's way, or shape, etc. Upon reviewing the components of the definition, one can say everyone has a job. We all have some sort of work to do no matter what our age. For example, let's start at the youngest age—an infant or newborn. Its job is to eat, sleep, and make a variety of pleasant sounds and gestures (smile, make cute, little cooing sounds), and unpleasant (puke and defecate) bodily functions, and to grow. This is a pretty basic job. An older child's job is to go to school and complete other assigned tasks such as chores, and follow the rules for whatever activities they're involved in. Adults jobs are multiple. For one, occupation; two, raise their families; and three, maintaining their property and possessions. For adults, these are the basic three. As you can see, it will take quite an exorbitant amount of time and lots of energy to perform them. These examples are simplified to just give you an idea and to define work components briefly. For each stage of life has its work, and is as complex as is each individual.

Many of us have few jobs in comparison to the next two areas of activity as you will see. The next division of activities that we will take a look at will be:

Chores. Webster's dictionary defines it plain and simple as follows: a small routine task as of housekeeping or farming, and as a hard or unpleasant task. It is no wonder it is like pulling teeth for most of us to get the chores done. Now comparing with the previous paragraphs on the definition of our jobs/work in life, where we are looking at maybe just a handful of things we are responsible for. How many chores are there? Depending on where we live and what we do, you can probably write a book on just chores. The never-ending list of things that need to be done just to maintain the home, never mind your property, equipment, family, and so forth.

REALMS OF ACTIVITY

The third division of activities that we will take a look at will be play.

Play. Now this is right up my alley. The term play is the largest definition in the dictionary. We will explore this in much greater detail later. It is the essential element to health, happiness, and contentment. It is the act of participating, as well as defined in the other two divisions work and chores. It's free movement, activity engaged in for enjoyment, to pretend, to manipulate ourselves or others or things, to act in a specified way. I think you get the idea.

We must consider activity as defined in each of the three divisions and in that particular order of which they have been listed. We must do so harmoniously and correctly to help us achieve productive balance.

When and if you wish to develop what I refer to as an *action plan,* which is simply a plan of your time structure. We will need to incorporate the things that you need to do for yourself in these three realms of activity work, chore, and play. In my training sessions I will also define life's activity in another way: as things we have to do, things we need to do and things we want to do. As we look at the activities and opportunities of life in this manner, we can use these divisions as a good starting point to develop our *Action Plan.* This not only gives us direction, it also gives a firm foundation to build on.

Let's look at these three divisions of activity.

Activity—Things you have to do. there are not many of these; there are only five basic behaviors:

- Sleep,
- Consume (eat, breath),
- Defecate (getting rid of our waste from consumption),
- Mate (Reproduce), and
- Play

These are the only five things you have to do to survive:

- We have to *consume* food, water, oxygen etc.;
- We have to *defecate*, bodily waste, etc.;

LIFESTYLE MANAGEMENT

- We have to *sleep*, rest, and recuperate;
- We don't have to *mate*; we are here. If this doesn't happen, our species will cease to exist; and
- We have to *play* to move, to think, to learn, and to react to stimuli.

Play is the only psychological behavior, the others are biological.

These are definitely basics. If you take away any of these or don't take care of them, you won't be around long enough to worry about anything else.

— *Things you need to do* - These are the chores in our life, personal hygiene, jobs, and home/property maintenance. There are tons of need-tos, in our life. If we don't take care of them next and schedule appropriate amounts of time for them, we will not have the means to live comfortably and do the want-tos.

— *Things you want to do* - If there are a thousand things we need to do, there are two million things we want to do. These are the *very things that make life and living a pleasure. The things that refresh us physically and intellectually, and keep the life cycle going.*

These are the first things you must take care of and incorporate into you time structure—*action plan.*

If we, at any time in our lives, do not take care of them or don't do our job(s) well (caring for ourselves and all that entails while performing our occupation /work), we won't gain in health, wealth or means to function at a level we wish to exist.

If each or any of us at any time in our life, do not take care of the many chores we need to do to maintain our property or family, both suffer. The property deteriorates and loses value instead of gaining it. The same goes for the family, as well.

We have seen this happen all over the country and world. With families not committed to each other and doing the necessary task for

REALMS OF ACTIVITY

each member of the family unit to grow healthy, strong and thrive, the family unit breaks down and separates.

If any of us, at any time in our life, did not take the time to play, to reach a state of refreshment and renewal, which is imperative in keeping the whole cycle of life going. Our life cycle from birth to death is dependent on refreshing and replenishing ourselves in all areas of our life at regular intervals. Whether the need be physical, social, emotional, or spiritual, choosing the right activities to incorporate into our lifestyle at the proper time becomes a key factor for this rejuvenation to happen effectively. This will help greatly to maintain an effective wellness level.

Let me put it like this! For the normal adult, *work* gives us the means to live at a specific level of comfort we choose. *Chores* keep us maintained, as well as our family and our homes/property. If we don't, we have to earn more to hire someone else to maintain and care for the stuff that we have. That also goes for our physical and mental health, as well as our property. *Play* is the time for us to refresh, become reenergized and vibrant, and to keep the life cycle going productively, not to mention making life an enjoyable journey.

Take care of all three divisions of activity in that order and you will have already begun to get yourself on track for the healthier life.

Chapter 5

Breaking Down Activity

My research and professional development programs in post college years led me to hunger for evaluation tools. There are too many to mention. I will have you use components of some surveys and exercises throughout this book to help you gain greater understanding of yourself and your makeup.

Early in my career working for a large community mental health center, I attended a postgraduate program offered by the University of Maryland called the Therapeutic Recreation Management School. It was a two-year program in which many professionals from around the country, as well as speakers from a variety of colleges and universities, came together for a few weeks at a time. They were leaders in their field from all over the country. It was held at a beautiful resort area in West Virginia. It was here where I found many of the tools that I started with and expanded on over the years. It was also here where I found some of the best categorization of activities at that time or have yet to find since. I believe it came from research and data compiled from North Texas University at the time.

I found the breakdown of activity categories and activity classification thorough. I have found it to be very useful in helping to identify whether or not one has balance in their life via involvement in the activities which they partake in on a regular basis.

Let's review each of the activity categories they had identified. I will explain what is entailed for each category. There were six categories identified, or should I refer to them as classifications of activity? Over the years I've attempted to expand the categories with each attempt coming to the conclusion that there was no need to break down any further. I believe this activity classification came about in the mid-1970s. Any activity that existed prior to or devised since then can still very easily be placed in one of the six original activity categories, which I will share with you now.

Let us look at these activity classifications or categories, and as we do so, I'll briefly describe each in reference to the types of activities that would fall within each specific category. Note the fact that one's involvement in a particular activity from any one category may encompass components of other categories when performing the activity.

One activity area is referred to as *creative*. To define this term using Webster's dictionary, the meaning consists of the following: to create, cause to happen, make, cause to be, bringing to life, make anew, etc.

Something to keep in mind is, there is an action requirement attached to this category. As you can see from the definitions, as well as with all of the activity categories, one must be engaged in an activity at a certain level of intensity to benefit from the activity experience. Hence, we will use the term *creative expression*. Creative expressive activity allows us an opportunity to coordinate and set the mind and spirit in motion. This guides our hands, words, and actions of our inner self. We can be creative in so many ways and through so many activities.

I have had athletes tell me they express their creativity on the playing field, on the court, or in their practice arenas. Not always to the delight of the coaches, I might add. Painters express through their art, musicians their music, writers their poems, stories, and articles, actors through their performance. I could truly go on indefinitely and fill volumes with the creative acts shared with me by my patients, clients, students, and individuals over the years. Each of us has unique talents and a unique creative way of expressing it to ourselves and others. Of course, we may even through our work express our creative gifts. The wonderful thing about creative involvement in our lives is that it gets us out of the routine, mundane, boring ritualistic aspects of our life—that day in and day out routine we all go through day after day. It gets us out of the rut(s) that our daily routine tends to dig us into.

Thinking a new thought would be the creative process, doing something we have never done before is a creative act. Just thinking of ways to identify creativity is refreshing to the mind, and a mind cleansing experience. I have found this activity category will often give us repeated payoffs well after the activity has been completed.

I will explain by taking you through a little memory stroll. To get ready for this I want you to take a few moments after reading the next few paragraphs, of course, clear your mind. Now scan your memory banks, and focus on something that you made at some point in your life. Something you made, and when it was done, you had a finished object of some sort. Something that others in the world could actually see, touch, hold, smell, or taste.

Stop.

Now, scan the memory banks, which I hope are full of these treasures, and select the one thing.

Chose the one thing that stands out in your mind the most; just one. Which one did you select? I bet you're smiling about it, aren't you?

Now, I want you to see yourself in your mind's eye when you are working on that project. Get ready to put the book down. Remember how you felt and what you were thinking while you were working on the project. I bet another smile and a twinkle in your eye just occurred.

I want you to remember while you are working on that item when you were actually performing the necessary task during the creating phase. I am willing to bet that you were focusing only on the activity at hand as the creative juices flowed. During your participation in this activity you selected, you had moments of limited or no distractions, possibly experiencing blissful periods of relief from whatever else was going on in your life at home, school, friends, etc. During the time you were actually working on the project, you had moments when you were oblivious to the time. Time may have even

BREAKING DOWN ACTIVITY

gotten away from you. Do you recall the excitement when you were working on that task? Creating that item, that project? Was there any anticipation when it was done that someone else would see it? Were you thinking about when the next time, next session, you would have to work on it?

Now, I want you to recall that day you finished. The moment you finished! When it was completely finished, remember the thoughts you had, how you felt, the very moment it was finished. The *Ah!* moment. "It's done." We always get a great feeling when we work in earnest and finish something to our satisfaction and that of others. Completing anything thoroughly is a growth experience. We all need to experience this occasionally, to reconfirm our value and worth in order to keep us moving forward in life.

Remember the sense of accomplishment, the sense of satisfaction? Now, remember when someone else saw it for the first time? What did they say? Was it a friend, teacher, family member? If you are one of 99.8%, you are smiling broadly right now because you were praised openly for your efforts and you can see their reactions as they looked at, touched, or tasted it; that very item you just created.

We are not done yet!

Do you remember when you took it home or showed it to others? What did they say about what you had done? Or better yet, you gave it to somebody as a gift? Remember the look in their eyes and expression on their face. When they opened it and realized that *you*, yes, *you* made that.

Reminisce and experience those moments which may have long since passed for at least a few minutes.

Now put down the book.

Yes, you remember the joy, the praise, and thankfulness! Part of you was in that item. That gift was part of you! You created a treasure for someone important to you. You created a treasure in your own heart because you know it came from your time, your thoughts, your efforts. Your actions are what caused it to be. That is impossible to buy for someone. You created it! *Wow*, that is pretty awesome, I think!

LIFESTYLE MANAGEMENT

Heck, we are not done yet!

Of course, we can be creative in so many ways as I mentioned earlier. One other important aspect of finished projects or products—it tends to bring us personal gratification. We may keep getting pay-offs long after the fact. For example, the particular object you just reminisced about or maybe other things you have made for yourself or a loved one, where is it displayed? Is it in a prominent spot?

Let's imagine or do you remember a time when you had a guest over? Someone new sees that item you made for the first time and admires it. The recipient of that item says something to the effect, "My daughter/son/friend/ (whatever your relationship may be to that person) made that for me." If you're in earshot of the comment or the person tells you of the experience, you are once again getting payoffs. You feel the joy, pride, gratification, a satisfaction inside for having pleased someone from an activity or an object you created years ago. Without saying a word, doing anything different, or in addition to, your spirit is lifted.

How do you feel, when you hear those compliments? When the recipient of the gift or object you created or the new admirer of the object has made those comments and you hear them, what goes through your mind? That old thing you made, let's say, fifteen years ago. Pretty cool, huh? And I bet you are acting very modest. Although inside, your personal sense of self is being inflated and you're thinking, *Oh yeah, I did that.*

For the moment and several after, you are energized, alert, a bit more self-confident, and at the very least, feeling some of the same gratification you felt and experienced years ago when you first made the item. Yes, you can admit it has happened more than once with that same object!

We don't often give ourselves compliments for a job well done. We are more often in situations that it's our job at work or a home responsibility where we consistently are doing a great job. Yet not ever getting praised or recognized for doing it. At least, we get our paychecks from work. At home, we don't even get that.

This is why it is so beneficial to allow ourselves opportunity at regular intervals to experience and express our self in our own unique and creative ways. By doing so we indirectly allow others to compliment us on our talents and openly acknowledge what we have done. We all need thanks and feedback occasionally, especially the good kind which comes from our creative acts. It is these acts which originate from within us that allow others a glimpse of our personal depth. This type of activity helps bring to the surface our inner workings, gifts, talents for others to see and acknowledge. It allows others to see our real self, confirm and hopefully praise. This affirmation, inspires us to strive do more, do better and encourages us to improve. The payoffs are great!

This doesn't mean there will not be some failures; this doesn't happen with every effort. Many of my projects over the years have become kindling and firewood. But all is not lost, for with any creative process, any earnest effort has potential to be purposeful. You know what? Even that firewood can create a warm, cozy fire to sit beside one cool evening when I'm alone or with someone I love. That is nice, also!

You see how creative thinking and expression can lead to many wonderful alternative ideas.

When we can express ourselves and explore our creativity regularly, it keeps us out of the rut of our ritualistic lifestyle we all tend to grind ourselves into. Once our habits and the routine of our lives get so ritualistic, the ruts get ever so deep. When this happens, we can only see the walls we have created around us. When we look ahead or behind, all we see is the same path, not the options and alternatives. Isn't that scary?

The routines we get ourselves into tend to keep us stuck.

So be creative.

Let's see the rest of the world and the possibilities outside and within. (That would take a creative act).

Let us now explore *intellectual* activity. Anything requiring thought, pretty simple, cut and dry!

Not so fast! True, some mental processes must occur before we do anything within this realm of activity. Whether it is a conscious decision or unconscious decision, our brain is the center, the processor of our central nervous system. Some action, reaction, chemical stimulus triggers a response, causing the body to do biological or reactionary effects, internally which may lead to external responses.

As long as we are alive and have our own ability to think, we have potential to stimulate our mind and body. Only when the brain is dead does this realm of activity no longer exist within our capabilities.

The brain's potential is amazingly vast. I have always found the topic of the brain so fascinating. The mind—a great curiosity still! The brain can be thought of as a vessel or the organ housing the workings of the mind. Let us say, the ignition switch that activates the body to do whatever it's supposed to do or perform whatever task needs to take place.

The mind! Now, there is another beast! The mind may not hold biological limits. Let's explore this concept of the mind for a moment. Let's say, "a meeting of the minds, of sorts," sharing thoughts, ideas, concepts, theories, and eventually, stimulating processes that may cause or lead to new discoveries and/or developments of something new. (Oops, that would be a creative act!)

By using and challenging our intellect, we begin to understand and see things differently, in a new light of other perspectives. All of which may lead to new ways of doing things, new activity, new cure for a disease, or a new technological breakthrough, and even the advancement of oneself, family, community, and society, where all may benefit. It is easy to get carried away with the vastness and limitless aspects of this activity category.

It is interesting and exciting to think of anything so limitless.

Yes, I know you probably are thinking of *God*.

Well, we were created in his image!

In God's great wisdom, we were given this potential, as limitless as it may seem. We are stuck in our ability and knowledge of how to tap into and use it to its maximum potential. Maybe that is part of the plan; to let us use only what we are really ready for. Could it be our own nature which is the real, limiting factor? That is one subject I'll leave to you to ponder.

It has always been my contention that if someone can do it, then anyone can do it, provided they have the ability to think and process, and if someone was willing to teach them in the manner for which the individual learns best. Also, if the individual was willing to learn, anyone can learn to do anything anyone else can do. Yet we may all learn differently and at different rates and we all have different levels of intelligence.

Some may have ability to learn and understand in ways no one else may.

So simply, the activity category of intellectual stimulation is basically any activity requiring thought and decision-making processes. In a sense, activity that stimulates the mind.

Now, let us explore another of the six: *physical exercise*. When most of us hear this, we may think of jogging, swimming, cross-training, or multiple activities requiring exertion, sweat and labor, and heavy breathing. Its definition includes sports of course, training, exercise routines. In a nutshell, any activity requiring movement.

As we go further into the lifestyle management process, I will make reference to *excessive physical exercise* or physical involvement. This is simply anything above and beyond our normal daily routines.

Keep in mind all the physical involvement we do throughout the day. From the moment we get up, we move all of our major muscle groups just getting out of bed, then following our morning mundane but necessary practices and rituals to get all ready for work, church, school, or just readying our self for our daily routines, getting dressed, groomed etc. Preparing our meals and snacks, moving about our home, going to the store, taking care of the business we need to do just to maintain our existence, all require movement.

We are involved in physical activity throughout the day. Even when we are sleeping, we are moving our body. Sleep research studies show that the average person will have more than 400 major muscle movements throughout the course of a night's sleep. It's no wonder we wake up in the morning feeling exhausted. We may have moved more during the night's sleep cycle than we have all day.

Each of us, if we are given the assignment, can easily identify one hundred different activities that we do throughout the day that require movement. Unless, of course, we are extremely ill or comatose.

LIFESTYLE MANAGEMENT

Have you ever been referred to or know someone who has been referred to as a couch potato. If you have you or they may have experienced that morning fatigue phenomenon from all the physical movement you were not even aware of that you performed all night long while you were asleep. Have you ever woken up and felt exhausted?

There's a world of physical activity and a fitness industry worth billions of dollars. They are pushing wellness with the major focus on this realm of activity. The sports industry encompasses every age group, starting with infants' programs and working through every stage of life to our death. Organized activities are starting shortly after birth, with things like water baby classes, peewee sports, little leagues, pre and middle school, junior high and high school, travel teams, colleges and universities, adult leagues, professional and senior Olympic sports.

I have my opinion of excessiveness with all the activity areas, especially in this physical exercise category. It is pushed on some, and in many cases, expected and forced upon some which may limit time that we have to focus on other aspects of life and growth as individuals. Yes, we all need to move to keep ourselves healthy, our body strong, useful, and functioning properly and efficiently.

Through many years of research, study, and observation, I have found that we, the human species, seem to be the only creature that participates in this activity category above and beyond what is necessary to survive.

I have come to the realization many years ago that the human body's potential is remarkable, to say the very least. To this day, on the sports scene, each year, human physical performance records are broken. We are getting stronger, faster, and jumping longer and higher distances than man ever has before. With the upcoming Olympiad, we will see this again. My conclusion is that humans, unlike other creatures, are made for movement!

What?

This is definitely a thought we should consider, and definitely one to contemplate on. Look at the average person—the design and shape. Look at our body's design and frame. Now compare that to a cheetah. Compare the frames of each. How cheetah's body stretches and flexes, it functions in such a way as to be designed for speed. Take a look at a falcon and other birds of prey. Their body frames are designed for flight, sleekness, and aerodynamics. These two examples of body are designed for a specific purpose. I believe that speaks for itself. Look at the many species of fish in the sea. Talk about being streamlined for purpose and shaped for specific movement. It's all so interesting and is fascinating, really, to watch and study movement and purpose of body design. So look at all these creatures mentioned. The ones you may have seen when you watched those TV specials about nature and various species of animals, birds, and fish.

Now, look at the human body. Humans are made for movement? We are not sleek nor aerodynamic in design. We don't have feathers for flight, gills to swim underwater, or four legs to run, yet we do these things.

Consider this: Out of all those creatures, which ones spend hours a day and much of its resources and energies to be able to perform at peak levels physically?

Only man!

Have you ever studied or observed animals in their natural habitat? Or watched them on the nature specials on TV? Well, have you ever seen one of these creatures exercising? What about lifting weights, doing chin-ups, attending spin class, or doing a daily five-mile jog? Of course not. Other than honing the skills, they have learned by watching parents which they will need to survive and practicing them until they reach maturity, they appear to move for that which is only necessary. Naturally, their instinctive forms of play are basic to their skills which will enhance their ability to survive in their natural environments. For all creatures other than man, it appears that all they must do, once they have reached maturity, to be well-maintained and in a high degree of health, fitness, and strength is *eat*.

You don't see them training every day. Oh, their typical daily routines may require movement. Only that which is necessary for the hunt and the capturing of its next meal and, of course, that which is necessary to continue the species. Humans, on the other hand, must move effectively and efficiently throughout our lives. When we don't, well, imagine if we just eat. Our bodies will lose their integrity and ability to move effectively, and the body loses its ability to function properly.

The Lord only knows what fish, amphibians, and other species do when they don't eat for extended periods of time. Let us not forget hibernating creatures and how they survive during their extended periods of hibernation and physical dormancy. I'm sure some scientists have figured it out.

What becomes apparent is that all other forms of life need to do is to eat regularly and groom (fur, feathers, scales, whatever they have) to stay in peak condition. For certain, there are oddities in nature that don't fall into the norm. On the other hand, what happens to humans if all we do is eat?

Instead of being in peak form, our muscles weaken. We have to move and move often and do what I refer to as excessive movement to maintain and enhance our healthy physical being. We also experience extra benefits from excessive movement. Remember, when I speak of excessive, I'm referring to anything above and beyond our basic daily routines as I mentioned earlier—beyond doing our chores, jobs, and the related movements that are required to perform all those repetitive tasks. When you think about it, we move a lot. Consider all the small movements we do over and over again, day in and day out. Despite lots of movement, unless we do other movements at regular intervals other than that of our typical daily activity, we can become more prone to injury or fatigue to specific areas of our body which may often lead to injury.

In the many years working in a pain clinic, I have found that many people will develop back pain and spinal injury from such continuous, repetitive movements over great periods of time required to perform their jobs. I have seen this time and time again. The reasons of the injury vary, but what is overwhelmingly consistent is that the repetitive movements required for the task at work compromises our body's integrity.

Our physical being is truly a remarkable thing.

We have all heard stories and probably read documents and research articles about people doing unbelievable things physically. In states of emergency, when the adrenaline flows, now being referred to as hysterical strength, ordinary people do extraordinary things—stories of a little lady from Georgia lifting up a vehicle and pulling the body of her grandson out from under it or the man doing a similar act at an accident scene in Tucson, AZ.

This goes back to biblical times with stories of Samson. Since the dawn of history, the body has done and is still doing unbelievable things in certain situations. The physical being and its potential, which seems to be limitless, appear to be only limited by one's vision and spirit. Of course, by design and nature, our bodies age as all things will. Nature takes its course, although many choose to battle against nature and the natural aging process. Many spend fortunes and much time in an attempt to counteract the inevitable. Surgeries can replace or inflate body parts (hips, knee, other organs, etc.), face-lifting, hair dying, stomach stapling, breast/butt implants, etc. So many of us don't want to age gracefully. We will fight nature, time, and the natural process of life, attempting to hold on to an image of ourselves which no longer exists.

Why fight that which is inevitable?

It is true, exercise in proper amounts and appropriate exercise for one's age and condition can help maintain a more healthy life and a more fit body. However, excessiveness at certain stages of our life can be and is damaging. We must be careful.

I divert from the benefit of physical exercise. I must state, I have never been a proponent of organized youth sports for a couple of reasons that I will focus on for the readers consideration I take this stance mainly due to the fact that it may affect your children or someone you may be close to. One of those reasons focuses on chronological age versus biological age, along with the social and physical development of an individual. Children are going to just naturally grow and do so at different rates and amounts. Oh, they can predict growth. Still, time and one's natural biological makeup will produce what it will in its own time.

Our physical intelligence is quite different from our social and emotional intelligence. For the most part, they all come around naturally about the same time, give or take a few months or years.

When driven by the cultural environment and we force our youth into certain activities, it can and does disrupt the natural developmental rhythm of the individual. This will be more thoroughly discussed in depth in chapters to come. The given culture in which we live, in many cases, encourages us to force our youth into activities with others that they may or may not be fully prepared to do physically, socially, or emotionally. When this happens, they are expected to perform at a very similar level as everyone else in that particular activity. This can be detrimental in many ways for the future of that individual's life and the choices and course they may take.

We have all seen this happen. A youth, who is very large for his age, is expected to play football. He is much bigger than all the other children, though he may or may not be coordinated enough to perform well. Or the very small child, who is very coordinated for his age, gets to participate with those much bigger and older. Another phenomenon that I've seen happen many times with youth sports, is the preparation and practice sessions. When training begins so early on in the young person's life, a few things happen.

First, after many years of training, by the time they are reaching their peak of strength and growth, they have already grown tired of the activity. They lose interest and may never actually live up to their maximum potential in whatever given sport or athletic event they were forced into too soon for whatever reason.

We grow and evolve through several distinct stages of play in our first fifteen years of life. Each stage is unique, different, and takes on different characteristics, all of which the individual is ready for at that particular time. Their time, not society's, coaches', or parents' time.

Each set of skills, when fully developed at each particular stage, gives us the prerequisites we need for the next stage as we grow and continue to develop. When we disallow that natural process by forcing our little ones through a particular stage too quickly, they may never fully develop the necessary skill set which is unique to that particular stage of development. This may very well affect some components of self, as well as one's character shaping, that only happens during associations and experiences at certain impressionable phases of our life.

BREAKING DOWN ACTIVITY

In some cases, the particular stage may only last a few months in their young lives. Let me add this; My experience has proven that it's very difficult—nearly impossible—to go back and retrace a particular stage and experience the unique things associated with that particular stage. Thus, the individual moves through our societal system to the next stage of their life without the necessary skills having been developed effectively to prepare them for this present stage socially, emotionally, mentally, and physically. *Something is always missing which can and does affect our psyche.*

Secondly, organized sports force children at a very young age into other rigid environments that are very structured. Specific skills need to be taught at a specific time. Thus, natural physical development may not take place due to the fact that specific musculature may be used excessively to perform the specific sports task. The repeating, over and over and over of the specific task is a necessary part of the training to perfect and develop the task/skill for functional use during the specific sport.

It's easy to see the dilemma and how overtraining can hinder the natural developmental process of the human body. Much research as of late has been recognizing injuries occurring in youth sports, especially when year-round training takes place or when extended periods of time are being spent with specific training task. Are we putting our youth at risk?

I think so! They are sustaining injuries that, years ago, only the most elite athletes and professionals would experience. It's no wonder kids escape to Game Boys, Play Stations, Xbox, Wii, computers, cell phones, etc. and isolate themselves from the joys and wonders of childhood—to be able to just run, jump, and play with kids their own age. It is always a pleasure to see kids get together on their own and to observe what they will do naturally. You guessed it. They play around. Do you remember their jobs at this stage outlined in chapter 4? They enjoy each other in healthy and natural ways. When you put a bunch of children in a room, on a field, or a playground together, they don't have to be told what to do. The interaction comes naturally if the development process(es) are not disrupted.

LIFESTYLE MANAGEMENT

Don't get me wrong. I enjoy sports and the competitive nature of sports, and I have all my life. I recognize the importance of sports and competition on our own physical/social well-being. Although I would much rather see our youth in their first twelve to thirteen years of life, play for the pleasure of being and interacting with their friends, doing so with no rule makers, regulations, and no one there to correct, discipline, or force them to do something repeatedly if a mistake or error is made. Give them a chance to interact freely to solve their own problems and dilemmas when something occurs. Let them learn each other's role and yes, fight their own battles and resolve their own problems and conflicts.

I may be speaking now of an era that has long since gone by. I acknowledge the need, due to the society in which we live, for safety and supervision of an adult, parent(s), or responsible party to watch and make sure that children are safe to play as they please.

This really shouldn't be too much of a problem. Despite everyone's busy schedules, how many parents, grandparents, neighbors, or nannies are usually just sitting in the parking lot or in the bleachers watching the coach drill, yell at, and discipline their young ones, waiting to take them home?

It might be more pleasant for all to watch their young ones, just play and see how their children solve their own problems and deal with adversity when given a chance. It would be way less expensive, less time consuming for many, and way less stressful on all involved.

I remember when the son of good friends of our family started high school. He was athletic and a well-developed lad due to all the outdoor and nature activities they did with their family throughout their developmental years up to this point. I asked him if he was going to go out for any sports. He just matter-of-factly said no.

When talking to his parents later and asking why he was not since, he was an outstanding ballplayer as a youth (both their sons were).

The mother shared this, which I thought was classic.

We will call him John. John wanted to play football and baseball because his friends did and they wanted him to. He went to a few practices and just decided not to play high school sports.

She said, when she asked him about it, he simply replied, "Why? Why would I want to go run, exercise, get all hot and sweaty, tired, out of breath, and get yelled at for two or three hours after school every day? When I come home, I am so tired. I can't eat. Then, do my homework and go to bed. When after school, I can go to Grandma's, get my homework done, and eat hotdogs and snacks. Then go do what I want to and have fun with my friends." Made perfect sense to me!

Life is too short!

Let's get back to the benefits of this activity category. We experience many benefits from *appropriate physical activity*. We become more alert, sleep and feel better. We are less prone to injury, sickness, or disease. We maintain proper body weight. We have greater energy levels. Plain and simple, we are better, look better, feel better, and have a greater sense of well-being.

Of course, the opposite is true when we don't exercise regularly or get enough physical activity in our life.

Another activity category—*social interaction*. This activity category, as all the others, has multiple perplexities. It also holds a unique (that's the wrong word), inquisitive (no that is not the right word either), let's say, an intriguing fascination for me. In college, I kept taking sociological study courses. Three were required for my major. The more I took the more interested I became. I found the whole topic of sociology and social development of our species a fascinating subject matter. We'll talk more about that later.

Let us explore social interaction. Everything we know, we learned from others. Whether it was through someone teaching us, showing us, observing others, or reading what others have written. I believe we are born with instincts. Some may refer to them as our subconscious and others our guardian angel. Whatever you may decide to call it, or how you choose to interpret it, this inner self or innate awareness is up to you. Whatever it is, I will refer to it as *instincts*. Our instincts are designed and geared to keep us out of trouble and out of harm's way. We see it in all nature's creatures. Their senses, sight, hearing, smell, and taste let them know and interpret the warning signs, and they stay clear of harm's way.

LIFESTYLE MANAGEMENT

My theory is, as humans we learn so much through our teachings, observations and interactions with others. We get so far beyond basic survival processes that, for the most part, we don't even know how to interpret or acknowledge our instinctive intelligence. Thus, we get ourselves into lots of trouble socially. This we will explore in the chapter devoted to the *desocialization* process.

We are the most socially complex creatures on God's green earth. I enjoy watching the specials on television highlighting the study of a specific animal species in some remote environment on the planet. I appreciate the work and research which went into such programs. At the end during the credits, the narrator ends his/her spiel with a final statement that goes something like this, "By further study and learning of the social behaviors of the Spotted Spider Monkey, we may come to a greater understanding of our own human nature."

That always kills it for me. It always makes me laugh every time I hear it. The species being studied may change, but the quote is the same. It would make perfect sense, if we were striving to catch up to the spider monkeys socially, emotionally, or intellectually. If that were the case, then maybe the spider monkeys would be studying us.

I have my theory on that one also, but I would not want to offend anyone. Plus, I do enjoy watching those programs and appreciate the sacrifice researchers make to learn about the creatures they study.

The *social category* of activity consists of and includes any activity that causes people to come together to partake in it. Let us explore the benefits further, other than what we already mentioned just briefly. We should start by looking at the most basic. Our species would not exist if two people did not get together occasionally to create more of us. As mentioned above any activity that brings us in contact with others to interact, share and participate with one another will fall within this category.

I heard a study recently on the radio while I was traveling, about this social media revolution. People are connected twenty-four, seven. One would suspect we are better off socially, getting our needs met, as well as meeting the needs of others. The studies are showing the opposite is true. The studies reveal that people connecting fewer times daily felt more connected and felt more secure in their relationships than those that are connecting more often with social media. The report also identified that those connecting with others forty plus times or more daily felt more isolated and fewer of their social needs were being met. Of course, I take most studies with a grain of salt; opinions and perspectives are as unique as each individual. We can and do find what we are looking for. Anything and everything is put out there.

There was a statement made by a lecturer many years ago during one of the management training programs I was required to attend as part of my professional development at a large Medical Center where I was employed. I quote, "Statistics don't lie, but liars can gather statistics."

So beware of what you read, see or hear!

When we were growing up, my father taught us many things. He would use parables and anecdotes, to teach us always use caution when listening to gossip and being a busy body. He would say, "Don't believe anything you hear and only half of what you see". And I must say he was way ahead of his time, that statement holds true today, even more so than it did 40 years ago.

We will discuss social needs further in chapters nine and ten, while we explore the socialization/desocialization process and why this social media statement may very well be true. Other benefits of social interaction are, well, basically as mentioned, the continuation of the species. I remember back in the seventies, when they were experimenting with what they referred to as the test-tube babies. Still, the egg and sperm had to come from human donors. I wonder how that ever turned out? Cloning, I guess. I prefer the old-fashioned way.

As mentioned, we learn from one another. Everything we need to survive or would want is brought about by the efforts of others. We go to a store to buy products, produce/food of all sorts grown by others, we wear clothes and adorn ourselves with items made from others' effort. We transport ourselves with automobiles, trains, planes, boats, buses, trolleys, ships, and such produced and operated by others. The switch we flip to turn on the light or to use the appliance as we do so liberally, the energy used is produced by someone at our power companies. We use fuels of the earth, wave action, and solar power, which are gathered, collected, and converted by someone somewhere, not to mention the workers involved, to make sure it gets to our homes. All are constantly maintained by others. Literally, everything we use was produced and touched by many others before it gets to or is available for each one of us. All of our needs are met by others in some way, shape, and form. We even, for the most part, get our own perspectives of self from how we are treated by others.

It is truly a rare individual who knows himself well enough that despite the feedback of others, can stand their ground and not falter in their dignity and/or self-respect.

Thank God for people like Job! That is a classic example of sticking to one's faith and knowledge of self and the righteousness of our heavenly Father. Way too often is the opposite case true, which will lead us into the next category of activity and the one that will help each of us achieve a greater sense of self, which I fear our society today is so much lacking. We are truly interdependent on one another!

Another activity classification is *solitary relaxation*. When exploring all the benefits of the other activity classification areas, what is left that we really need to survive with? What does this area of solitary relaxation entail? Exploring the word *solitary* means being alone, by and of oneself. The other component, *relaxation*—rest, relaxing, rejuvenation, recovery. I would also like to add, self-rediscovery! Basically, let us take a look at the body's, as well as the mind's need to relax, to let go, to rest. Sleep is a basic behavior. We explored the five basic behaviors in chapter four. We all need to rest and sleep—the body's most natural way to refresh itself, and might I add, to effectively heal itself. It is truly amazing, the body's potential in its healing ability when we ourselves don't interfere with this natural process and built-in capability.

Let me reference from the book of Psalms 139:14, "I will praise you for I am fearfully and wonderfully made; marvelous are thy works, and that my soul knoweth right well."

We fight this relaxation process continuously in so many ways. Yes, I am personally very guilty of this offense. I hinder myself and

BREAKING DOWN ACTIVITY

my ability and potential to get what I need from this one activity area. Hence many times messing up the opportunity to keep myself functioning at my best. We get so tied up in the doing, accomplishing, finishing of what task we have at hand and the activities of life. All noble and warranted objectives, I hope.

I mentioned earlier when exploring the creative expression category of activity, but it's worth repeating. The finishing of any activity is important. It puts a cap or an end to whatever the task, project, or assignment may be. Once finished, the internal and external message is *time to move on*, *go forward*, or time for something new—a new challenge, new goal, or a new beginning. We can and do become addicted to doing; this too must be guarded against. We will discuss this further in Chapter 6.

Believe me, I have spent a lifetime studying and processing activities from every angle. I took my profession as a Recreation Therapist very seriously. I have dedicated my life to the examining and understanding of specific components of activity. I have dissected them into specific movements, studying the various aspects of activities. I have explored the cause and effect they have on the individual, one's genetic potential, along with the social and emotional impact of activity. I have researched the activity origin. I spent much time studying activity association, in relation to and through one's developmental year's comparing chronological and development readiness.

I guess you can say, I'm an activity expert.

I will never know every activity, nor expect to. It has been a lifetime goal for myself and I wish for you also, to always explore activities when the opportunities come your way. I always tell my patients and clients whenever they have an opportunity to do something they've never done before, to do it. I always add, if it won't hurt them or anyone else, do it, even if you think you're going to hate the activity. You might find the next new activity you do, even though you thought you were going to hate it, may be something you enjoy immensely. You may find that you may never want to do it again. But at the very least, you have expanded your horizons and your awareness. So even that time was not wasted as you did gain more knowledge and more experience.

LIFESTYLE MANAGEMENT

I have found this to be true throughout my life. To this day, I wonder how my life or the course of it may have changed, for better or worse if I had this advice much earlier in life.

For my first twenty plus years, I was more concerned with presenting an image of what I thought I wanted to be. Therefore allowing myself to do only things which would enhance the image, not necessarily the true self. Since taking the advice myself, which I have given to my clients, patients, and anyone who would listen throughout my life. I have had so many pleasant, enjoyable, enriching and memorable experiences that I could share.

I wish this for you also!

On the other hand, you might find that the next activity you do, which you have never done before in your entire life, might be the thing that you can do better than anybody else. It might be the very thing you were born to do. It might be that special gift that you have always been intended to do, but for whatever reason were not exposed to, not interested in, nor inclined to pursue.

I recall from one of my postgraduate classes, I think it must have been one of the statistics classes.

We were exploring the fact that there are millions of activities. We were discussing it would be a never ending process attempting to identify them all. New activities are constantly being invented every day.

I recall wanting to emphasize this to the participants in one of my lifestyle management classes We were exploring potential resources at our fingertips that we can call upon anytime, anywhere we wish. I pulled a deck of cards out of my pocket, three quarters of an inch thick, two and a half inches wide and three and a half inches long. I asked the group how many activities we can do with this little resource—this deck of cards. Of course, they started naming different card games they had played and were familiar with, so I stopped them. What is the most common poker game known around the world? Everyone knows five-card draw. I asked how many variations are there to that one game. Answers began to ring out all around the room, and soon, at least fifteen different options for five-card draw were named. To save time, I would ask them how many cards are in the deck and if they ever played with a wildcard or two wildcards or changing combinations when a particular card shows up. It doesn't take long if you do the math, that just from this one game there can be over 250,000 options.

Let me reiterate just that one game. So literally, the number of different activities that can be done with just a single deck of cards is endless. That is just one little resource that can fit very comfortably in your back pocket.

Now try comprehending the number of potential activities and resources we have at our fingertips throughout every household, not to mention community, country, and the world. As I mentioned earlier, we will never exhaust our activity resource potential. We can only do so by choice or incapacity which may come in many forms. I have diverted once again as I may so often do when discussing the subject about lifestyle management and activity. Let us get back on track.

Where were we? Ah yes, solitary relaxation! At intervals throughout our life, it is necessary to incorporate and utilize this realm of activity. Might I add, it is imperative to do so, if you recall basic needs. We need to step back and to reflect on where we are, where we have been, and where we are going, to refresh, to let go, to recuperate, and to rejuvenate ourselves. A little bit of this category of activity (solitary relaxation) can and does go a long, long way. When we can take advantage of this type of activity in its purest sense and allow the solitary component (of oneself and by oneself), the benefit is amazing.

Imagine, if you can for a moment, especially in this world where many feel that we have to be connected twenty-four, seven, 365, if you were willing to let yourself go completely. Imagine taking time when you would decide to just be, even if for just a moment. Let's say one minute, ten minutes, or what about an hour? To be able to let everything go, to not even let yourself think, to be absolutely still and not even let the brain acknowledge or bring to be a thought, *could you? Would you?*

I know many of you are thinking this is not possible.

Some of you are saying sure, I can flip the switch, shut off the TV, radio, computer, cell phone, iPod, or whatever social media

LIFESTYLE MANAGEMENT

device(s) you have and are carrying with you. Or can you? Some of you are saying, "I do that every night".

How many of you keep the cell phone within arm's reach when you go to bed?

Aha, that's what I thought!

It is difficult to let go; even more difficult to empty ourselves completely of actions and thoughts. The recuperative potential is great when we can learn to do it even for just a few moments.

Many years ago, during my prime athletic phase of life, I studied and practiced various forms of meditation and relaxation techniques. Examples: transcendental meditation, yoga, guided imagery, the study of hypnosis, and many forms of concentration to enhance my psyche to better prepare myself for the physical and psychological readiness of competition. After my competitive years in sports were over, I found that now I needed to do this more as a stress reliever, and to maintain proper and healthy physiological effects. Example, lowering blood pressure and lowering heart rate. Oh yes, you can control some of your biological effects with proper mind use. We read about the many examples of this where people can do strange and remarkable things. There are even cases when surgical procedures have been performed without anesthesia.

I will share a personal experience. I happened to be in the emergency room on a Friday. The emergency room on a Friday night is no place to be if you are an impatient person. In the ER waiting for an MRI, I was in stable condition, in good spirits, and treated well. The medical staff following protocol had me hooked up to all the monitors to ensure everything was stable. The monitors are making sure I was maintaining safe levels of heart rate, pulse, and blood pressure. If I wasn't within a normal safe range, the beeping sound increased in speed and volume, alerting the nursing staff and medical staff and letting them know something wasn't right.

Everything was fine until the nurse informed me that an accident victim was coming in, and I would be bumped. Then there goes the monitors—*beep-beep-beep* loud and fast, as my anxiety and impatience increased. Forty-five minutes later, another siren. The nurse comes in again to say it would be another thirty to forty-five minutes: *beep-beep-beep*. After this happened a few times, I realized it was just me causing this rapid beeping to occur. "Mr. Gagnon, you just got bumped again." *Beep-beep-beep.*

The nursing staff patiently explained why it takes so long between MRI uses, the preparation after each use, the required cleaning, disinfecting, recharging, reviewing results before the next patient prep, etc. Now it was well past midnight and all I had to do is hear an ambulance and it would make the vital signs increase. So I decided to control myself, keeping my physiological and biological self under control. I'm encouraging my spouse to go home and assuring her I would be fine. She's steadfast and dutiful, despite my encouragement to leave. She stayed by my bedside. After another hour or so of the rheumatic and annoying beeping, boredom set in. Emergency after emergency, bump after bump. By now, I am livid.

I can think of many words and phrases to say to express what I was thinking. I won't do so for not wanting to offend my reader. Since I was not allowed to move despite the discomfort, I did not want to disturb my wife, who was dozing in the chair beside me. I decided to entertain myself. I decided to put this control thing to the test. So I decided, I would pass the time by seeing if I could cause the beeping to go faster. I started to think about the things I had not finished—some home projects which were overdue. *Beep, beep, beep.* Cool! In comes the medical staff. I would calm down and slow the beeping.

I began reviewing in my mind projects I had at work and deadlines, *beep, beep, beep, beep, beep!* I began to think when or if I could finish these projects and assignments. I began to wonder if I would be able to after this ordeal is over and done. *Beep, beep, beep, beep, beep!* That really set me off and made me anxious. Yes, *this is cool.* Let's play *control the heartbeat, blood pressure, pulse.* I was able to do so on command. Each time, it would wake my wife. Finally, I said, "Watch this." When she realized I was doing this, she told me to stop. She really got angry when the nurses would come in. Then, I decided to see if I can slow everything down since that didn't make a louder sound, all it did was change the length of time between each beep. This was not disturbing my wife, until she realized what I was doing. She made me stop that as well.

LIFESTYLE MANAGEMENT

Finally, at 3:00 a.m., I got the MRI. While waiting for the results, my spouse asked the plastic surgeon after he examined me, if I needed surgery and how long would take. His reply was, "He may be in surgery seven to eight hours. I will have to wait for the results of the MRI to be sure."

Finally, my wife agreed to go home at my urging to get some rest. Twenty minutes later, the surgeon comes back and tells me that no bones, teeth, or ligaments were broken nor shattered or damaged. He explains, "I have seen and worked on many similar cases. I didn't believe the x-rays, that is why I ordered the MRI and surgery preparation. I can't believe there is not more damage."

To my delight! I asked him, "So how long will the surgery be?" His response was "Fifteen to twenty minutes. I can perform all skin alignments and suturing right here."

Immediately, I tell the nurse and the doctors, "Don't call my wife. I would just go rest in my office and call her later."

The nurse said, "It is too late. She has already been called and she is on her way."

I was very lucky, and the Lord was with me and blessed me.

The whole purpose of sharing this experience with you was to let you know and give you an example of how we all have some capacity to control some parts of our physical and biological functions. Although this was one activity within this solitary relaxation category, performed in an unusual environment and circumstance. I would like to point out that you do not have to be an expert mentalist, hypnotist, or yogi, to perform such activities. As with any task or skill development, practice enhances and improves the outcome.

By letting ourselves, for short periods of time, not to be influenced by any internal or external forces and factors, we can allow ourselves to do seemingly remarkable things. When we learn we can allow such opportunities, even if just for a few moments to not think or feel, we are allowing ourselves to be free from inhibiting influences and factors. This will better allow our body and mind to find its own balance.

It is also important to know that when we allow ourselves to clear and recharge, recharging is truly what happens. You will find a peace and energy you never knew you had.

BREAKING DOWN ACTIVITY

Let us back up a moment as I don't want anyone getting the wrong idea. The mind control play I just shared with you—slowing and speeding up beeps—that was my doing. The miraculous and totally unexpected healing that occurred that night in the emergency room, so I did not need surgical intervention, was something much greater than my insignificant skill or powers of self-control could perform. I think the miracle took place moments after my injury. Once I realized what had happened, my first and immediate prayer was "Lord, however this turns out, may my appearance not be repulsive to my patients and people you wish for me to come in contact with and serve."

I have worked in psychiatric facilities, substance abuse centers, crisis units, and rehabilitation facilities over three decades. I had the privilege to work with many excellent therapists and doctors from several disciplines. I have found the best ones had no magic pill. Oh yes, the assigned physician wrote the proper prescriptions to help stabilize the patient. Along with that, the most effective psychiatrists were able to do something remarkable. They would ask questions, and eventually the right set of questions at the right time which would help the patient find the answers they already had within themselves. Yes, I believe the old adage, "Our greatest battles are fought within."

It is my hope the readers of this book will learn more about themselves than they ever cared to. With that knowledge, each will be able to make the best decisions to effectively manage their life along with being able to compensate for imbalances that will occur throughout their life.

I would like to share another experience with you, if you don't mind, which falls within the borders of this activity area. When I was blessed with this new knowledge (at least, new to me) about creating balance in one's life, I set out to start practicing what I preached. I would take the balanced lifestyle survey every six months or so to re-assess my balance or lack thereof. My weakest area was consistently *solitary relaxation*. So I gave myself a goal. That goal was: "I would do nothing once a week for ten minutes." I knew that would be difficult for me, at least, initially. I knew with practice I would get better at it.

LIFESTYLE MANAGEMENT

If someone, whether it be friend, family, foe, or colleague of mine, had said to me I would still be struggling with that goal a year from now, I would have thought that is absurd. I knew I would have mastered the art of doing nothing. I am thinking, a year from now, I will be doing nothing very well by then. After a year of practice, I'll be an expert at doing nothing, thank you very much!

Half a lifetime later, I still struggle with this activity goal. Throughout the last several decades, I have developed skills that I used in my practice, teaching others ways to do this and to relax and center themselves. As for myself, even now as in the past, I experience random and rare success with this goal. It's not that I couldn't get better at letting everything go for ten minutes for my own intent and purposes. When I do use the proper techniques and take the time to utilize them, I had some wonderful experiences. It was more of an issue of allowing myself time and to take advantage of the techniques. I was not giving myself permission to let go of the thoughts and anxieties, which created the need for the refreshing and centering of myself, even when it was imperative and necessary to do so.

Whether we believe it's selfishness or we do not want to miss anything, or in my case just wanting to get something else done, we don't use all the tools for ourselves as often as we need to. I knew from experience that I, as well as the patients and clients, will get much better at using the techniques with practice. When I take the time to effectively work or play at the process, I experience the marvelously refreshing and renewing qualities of the time spent involved in these activities. Thus, the expected outcome was achieved! We need to allow opportunity to *effectively* utilize this activity area. What so often occurs with many of us is, we let ourselves and our lifestyle be dictated by the task immediately at hand. This is so easy to do, especially in true emergencies and crisis situations where it may be necessary. But, Really, Seriously! How many true life and death emergencies are we faced with? Think about it. How many times, have you been in a predicament that if you didn't react at that instant, you or someone else would have died or been seriously injured? Unless, you are a paramedic, soldier, emergency room staff, or ER doctor, I would guess it's pretty rare. Rare indeed when you find yourself in a life or death situation.

I have seen, as I'm sure you have as well, managers who spend great amounts of time *putting out fires* in the workplace; their job being dictated by attempting to appease the employees they are responsible for. They are constantly dealing with personnel or department complaints. The department suffers from lack of efficiency. Or what about this one? Parents reacting and adjusting their schedules to meet the interests (notice I did not use the term *needs*) of their children. I could share so many professional and private examples of this that have been shared with me over the years. I could fill multiple texts, volumes, or start a new TV series entitled *Can you believe it?* or *What are you thinking?* Many of which boggle the mind and are beyond reason. At least, in my mind.

One such example I heard was about a teenage girl whose mother was out of town helping her parents—the girl's grandparents. The father, at work as a product sales representative, was on the road approximately an hour and a half drive away from home. He still had several scheduled stops to make before ending his workday. His daughter was constantly calling him, explaining she had to get to her friend's house, which was in the town of their residence. An approximately thirty-minute walk, if she chose to walk. The daughter explained there was no way of getting there, except that he come home immediately and take her. The purpose of this *emergency*, from what I gathered in our conversation, was a school project which needed to get done. Finally, after her great persistence and multiple calls, dad canceled his schedule and drove home in response to the demand!

I understand family and responsibility to family. My fear in such situations, which are wonderful teaching opportunities, is that we are teaching an unrealistic lesson. Let me explain! There is, for every action, a reaction—simple physics. For every decision of action, there is a consequence. When we learn that there is no consequence (other than our own expected outcome) for our actions or non-action, why would one ever adjust one's behavior even when it would be appropriate to do so? Life is full of change; it is a constant

LIFESTYLE MANAGEMENT

we must all learn to contend with. Throughout our life, we will need to make adjustments to manage our lives effectively. The sooner we understand this process and learn to adjust the better off we will be.

We learn important lessons about life, give-and-take, and responsibility for one's own actions. We experience how an action can affect others and ourselves. We learn what is reasonable and what's not. We learn how to consider the circumstances of each situation and what the consequences are for our actions or lack of actions for whatever tasks, assignments, or duties we have. We learn to be responsible and considerate of others! The lessons we learn by compromising, negotiating, and realizing our time and that of others is valuable will serve us well in life. We learn how to use resources, to meet our own needs, as well as the needs of others. This is so important when learning to get along in the world with others.

In a sense, basic personal and societal responsibility is a learned process. I find that more and more with each generation we become less effective at teaching personal and communal responsibility. We do what we want to do. If that doesn't suit you, oh well! We have a society running rampant doing whatever, whenever, wherever, with whomever.

Lawsuits are involving everyone whether or not they are involved. (Example, drunk driver causing an accident, the victim sues the drunk driver, the insurance company, tire manufacturer, maker of the automobile, the bartender at the establishment who served the individual, the highway department, etc.) No one wants to assume responsibility for their actions nor their behaviors. Instead, responsibility is denied. It is being placed anywhere, except where it belongs. Even more amazingly to me, my decisions and actions may even be determined not my responsibility and legitimized in some courts of law, if I am found to be under the influence of foreign substances or mentally ill. So let's make everyone responsible for everyone else; just not themselves. It's a frightening thought to see the direction our society is going.

Let us get back on track.

Stresses of life are killing and robbing us of the very life energy that allows each and every one of us to flourish and grow. To keep healthy, strong, and to enjoy the life we have been given, we need to incorporate activities from the solitary relaxation category at regular intervals into our lifestyle. My wish for all of us, is to grow and live in one's own peace. Within is the only place in this world we will find what we all seek—*peace*. You may want to reference John ch. 14, 27.

As mentioned earlier, a little bit of this activity category, *solitary relaxation*, beyond the basic requirement of sleep and rest, can and does go an awfully long way.

So grant yourself this—peace!

Last of the activity categories but certainly not least is *Spectator* type of involvement. Activities that fall within this realm don't require active physical involvement. We don't always have to be doing things. We learn from observing, watching, listening, even touching, feeling, tasting, and smelling; all are ways to observe. During participation in this realm of activity, you are not involved in the action, only in the observation, while others perform. A majority of our time is spent in this activity category. More so now than ever before, we have become a society, a world of spectators.

We crowd thousands into the sports arenas, into concert halls, and millions are tuned on to television and go to movie theaters, visit social network sites (SNS), and other social media devices to a fault. We can't always be physically, actively involved. It's fun and exciting to root for our favorite team, listen to our favorite musicians, go to the movies, or sit at a window and watch the snow fly or listen to the rain fall.

We travel halfway around the world to see a spectacular sight.

To hear the voice of a loved one or to see them is a most pleasing experience.

We listen to hear the birds sing and the wind blow.

Don't we love the smell of freshly baked bread or a lavender field after a gentle rain?

Can you smell the apple pie just pulled from the oven, or the fresh scent of pine in a mountain forest, or balsam wood burning in a campfire?

I think you get the picture.

Spectator type of activity involves one or more of the senses during the observation experience.

LIFESTYLE MANAGEMENT

There you have it. The six involvement areas, activity categories, activity classifications, or however you wish to refer to them. I have spent well over thirty-five years looking to find another classification for activity. As I mentioned earlier, I have yet to find another, for every activity I have found would comfortably fit into any of these categories of activities we just reviewed.

Let us conclude this chapter by briefly reviewing and summarizing the benefits of each of the activity categories:

Creative expression: experiencing oneself in unique personal ways, to make anew, or exploring new ground. We will get more personal gratification and more payoffs via feedback and sense of self in the long-term from this activity area.

Intellectual stimulation: expanding the mind, thinking, processing, decision-making. Before each and every action, a thought process takes place. We haven't even begun to understand the potential or limits of the human brain.

Physical exercise: bodily growth and development, movement, exerting, reducing stress, and tension of one's body, relief, improved health, strength, endurance, stamina, improved energy, improved sleep and rest. All are benefits of this activity area.

Social interaction: being and interacting with others. Learning all we know, needs gratification (food, shelter, employment, etc.) and perspective of oneself via support and feedback from others; continuation of the species. Plus, the pleasure and joy of being and doing things with others. Any time you add a person to an activity it enhances everything we do. Also, it will make it more interesting to say the least.

Solitary relaxation: sleep, rest, recuperation to refresh and rejuvenate oneself (mind/body and spirit). To think our own thoughts and feel our own feelings without distractions. To truly find who and what we are. Through this involvement area we can realize our purpose, the value of our soul and unlock our potential.

Spectator appreciation: to step back, observe, to not be in the action, just taking in and observing and absorbing what is going on around you without being on the firing line or in the mix. Just being in the immediate present, here and now. Stepping back on the action and enjoying a nonthreatening participatory involvement. Involving the senses and not the kinetic.

It's easy to see the importance of each of the six involvement areas. Each activity classification category offers each of us something unique to our existence and well-being. We all need to assess ourselves and determine whether or not we are getting what we so assuredly need from each category of activity. When we don't get what we need from each area, we do not have a balanced lifestyle. When we lack balance for extended periods of time, it affects us in so many ways. It can affect us physically, socially, emotionally, and psychologically.

My wish for all is that you find the balance you need and maintain it. So, as you go through this gift, this testing ground called life, you will live it productively.

Chapter 6

Limiting Factors

Now you have the basic knowledge and understanding of the various categories of activity which are the key ingredients necessary to create a balanced lifestyle. It will be our choice of activities, along with making appropriate decisions and adjustments, that will bring about balance in our life. By selecting when, where, what, and how to do the things, we need to do to create a more healthy, more productive, and hopefully, happier existence. So why not get started? If only it were that easy!

It is!

But, oh yeah, there is always a *catch*; always a *big but*. As my spouse would say years ago, *"That can be a wide subject."* True to form, she is always right. Or at least, most of the time. No one is perfect. Let me say, she's right 99.9% of the time.

My career as a therapist is specifically devoted to finding what will work best for the individual, bringing the best out of each individual and finding their gifts and talents, then attempt to optimize their potential at that activity(s). During my practice, I claimed the title Lifestyle Management Specialist. I have run into every excuse imaginable on why people can't do things that would allow them to live a productive, healthy, happy, enjoyable, more content, and gratifying life. In so many cases, people just don't know what will work for them for multiple reasons. Actually, in some cases, even when they do know what will work, they won't do the things needed and necessary.

Years of research, compiling data, along with working with thousands of people in a variety of treatment settings and in private sessions, in small, large groups, auditoriums, and individually, I have outlined many of the most common excuses leading me to what I refer to as *limiting factors*.

Limiting factors can and do present themselves in many ways, shapes, and forms. They are unique to each individual, for each individual comes with their own set of circumstances.

Although, too numerous to list, limiting factors can be internal or external. These things that interfere with our ability, or better yet, a more appropriate term to use would be willingness to make effective decisions about the involvement we choose. The activities that we would select under these delineations of time uses, **work, chores** and ***play***, will reflect and determine the productiveness of our lifestyle and impact our outlook on life. It may not always be easy to get involved and/ or started when attempting the incorporation of new activities into our lifestyle. There are many limiting factors we face daily—changes in our health, in our functional capacities, illness, disease, accident, or injury. They can be cognitive, developmental, and emotional, or as mentioned, a variety of other circumstances we happen to be facing at the time.

Some examples are, if someone has a stroke, brain injury, cardiovascular accident, bad habits, birth defects or mental retardation (developmental disorders), psychological illnesses, environmental issues, or when we find ourselves in areas that are geographically lacking a certain variety of resources. All the above examples can and do interfere with or may prevent us from making the most effective choices when it comes to managing our lives.

If you take a moment and consider all that these examples can encompass, you can see how numerous limiting factors could interfere with an individual's ability to make necessary decisions about selecting the options that may work best for them. I have been told of and have discussed many unique situations and circumstances. Many real and some unreal factors that could easily fill the book shelf. Many of which we can all relate to; some so horrific, one would not even want to imagine.

"Fact can be stranger than fiction."

In some cases, you only could wish it was fiction and limited only to one's imagination.

Through all, the very interesting cases I have had over the years, I have heard of so many unique limiting factors. I have determined although many things can stop or prevent us from making good choices about managing one's life. I found we can really break them down to three areas. These are what I refer to as the *three major limiting factors.*

No matter what it is you may identify that is limiting or preventing you from doing things you need and want to do, it will fall under one of these three major factors. One of which is *knowledge*. Once you know what is going to work for you, you do it, right? At least, it would be reasonable to think one would.

I've worked extensively throughout my career in a major hospital-based medical rehabilitation center. I have worked with many people with spinal cord injuries in their cervical, thoracic, lumbar, and sacral levels, with people who have normal functioning of their extremities to no use of their extremities. I've also worked with thousands of people who have suffered from the effects of stroke, traumatic brain injuries and people with hemiplegic symptoms. There were many with speech and language deficits, along with visual, cognitive, perceptual, and reasoning impairments.

This list can go on indefinitely. Even throughout nearly four decades of service and numerous diagnoses, new ones seemed to be added to the list each year. I'm sure the future will bring new technology, new awareness, new discoveries, new conditions, illnesses, and diseases finding their way into humanity. Throughout the course of my career, I have seen so many victims of the various limiting conditions. In so many cases, the victims and their families believed that they or their loved one would never be able to do certain things again. Yet with proper therapeutic training, modifications of specific activity and the gaining knowledge of technology and adaptive equipment, they soon realize they can do the activities that they had done before. They can pursue the activities (work, chore, and play-related) as effectively as ever, sometimes even better.

Let us look at some examples here. One is of me personally finding out upon taking a specialized course designed to teach people with different types of handicapping conditions to resume playing golf. I have never been a good golfer. I will play occasionally—at conferences, with colleagues, fundraising tournaments, just for fun. Just enough to know that I am not good at it. Although working in a rehabilitation facility, many patients I worked with did enjoy the sport. Many thought they would never get to play again after losing a limb or a lessening of other functional capability of various parts of the body. It was up to me to help them find ways they could resume the activities they enjoyed. Upon taking these adaptable clinics and workshops, I would learn various alternative approaches—how to modify swings and compensate for deficits of mobility. I learned the use of adaptive equipment available to assist individuals in every aspect of the game. I actually found I am a much more efficient putter using one hand/arm with a backstroke swing technique, standing with the ball on the outside of my right foot.

Driving the ball with one hand didn't give me the distance I needed, but I found it keeps my ball on the course. Instead of driving my balls into the parking lot, the roughs, or traps, I was more consistent staying on course with a straighter ball. I would not hit the ball as far. But fewer strokes were needed to complete the hole. Understanding the physiology, mechanics, and the kinetics of movements of the body, this made perfect sense to me, which I will not go into detail at this point, for this is just an example of how sometimes we can learn to do things differently and be better at the activity than we were before.

Another experience I would like to share, is the first time I brought physically challenged athletes to a national event they had qualified for. It happened to be in Atlanta, GA, where they hosted the Americas Wheelchair Track and Field Championships. All of the biggest names in adaptive sports were there. As one of our athletes happen to be preparing to compete in a field event, they were announcing the 1,500 meter participants lane by lane. The race starts, and after a very short period of time, the gun fires again announcing the final lap. I looked up at the clock, and only a little over two minutes had past. I thought the time clock was malfunctioning. I looked at one of the other therapists who was with us and said, "Here we are in this great stadium at a national event, and the clock doesn't work." After the last of the racers came in and the final times for each were posted on the big screen, I couldn't believe what I was seeing and hearing. Everyone in that heat finished the 1,500 meters race under three minutes and eight seconds.

I thought, "Wow, the fastest runner in the world could not have finished that race in three minutes and thirty seconds." Yet here, today, in front of my very eyes, eight people in wheelchairs (racing wheelchairs, there is a big difference) finished in three minutes and eight seconds. *Wow!*

How many times have I heard patients over the years say, "This may sound strange, but this is the best thing that ever happened to me." Sometimes they would add, "At least in many years." This is almost always referenced many years even prior to their injuries.

On the other hand, I have had many say, "If I can't do it right, I don't want to do it". Isn't the safest, most efficient way of doing something, especially if it enhances performance, the best way? This is a mindset people get into. I have learned not to debate with them, unless evaluated results had identified strong preference and potential in specific activity(s). Sometimes changes and adaptations can make life better, despite our self. It really depends on our outlook and attitude of acceptance, and playing the hand we are dealt to our best advantage. I do believe everything that happens in our life, even if at first glance appears terrible, is really an opportunity, and can be a Blessing. This I have also, heard and experienced many times!

The next examples are from a crisis intervention center and psychiatric facilities. Here is where the knowledge factor may assist an individual, also where limiting factors can take on other unique dimensions, such as an anxiety attack(s) provoked by one's own psychology when introducing or experiencing an activity. In this case, I am about to share with you a patient's experience with physical activity, which they had avoided nearly all their life.

LIMITING FACTORS

This may sound like a lot of people in our society, especially in the social media generation where the thought of exercise may provoke fear. Follow me now! Remember, when we were describing the benefits of physical activity? The term I used, *excessive physical activity*, which is anything above and beyond our daily ritualistic routines. As we know, any time we start an exercise program, our heart rates increase, blood pressure rises, our body heats up, we start to perspire, it becomes difficult to catch our breath, and breathing becomes deeper and labored—all the same physiological effects that kick in when someone is having a panic attack. Knowing our body's reactions to excessive activity, these are all natural reactions of the body during such activity. It means the body is working effectively and doing the natural things to supply the energy necessary to prolong the activity. The body moves from its hyperstatic state to an elevated level by heating up, perspiring, and breathing heavily to consume and use more oxygen, in order to replenish oxygenation requirements of the body to allow the activity to be continued—all healthy, natural bodily responses. On the other hand, that is the same symptomatology that one experiences when having a panic attack. Thus participation in such an activity causes the body to produce these physiological symptoms, provoking the individual into thinking they are having a panic attack.

The unfortunate fact is, the only reference this individual had to these symptoms were associated with panic attacks. Due to the reactions of their body, combined with their past experiences associated with these effects, they become fearful and will withdraw from the activity. The exercise session triggers the physiological effects necessary for the activity, for the individual who may have faced some traumatic experience may only associate these symptoms with threats. Despite the individual realizing they are in a safe environment and participating in a safe and beneficial activity, the anxiety becomes overwhelming. Thus, triggering an emotional response. The embedded knowledge, although in many cases a subconscious awareness, from an experience long ago, is buried within the depths of one's brain, memory bank, and psyche of which they associated something bad happening.

LIFESTYLE MANAGEMENT

The only awareness and emotion associated with these bodily effects, was of fear. When one experiences the bodily responses even though not associated with the threat, they may shut themselves down. It becomes obvious, whatever the threat or experience the individual had, that has caused it to be embedded in their mind, they associate those natural physiological symptoms and responses of the body to something fearful. When they experience those bodily responses, it triggers the emotion again and again. It doesn't matter what is causing the body to react. Something that may have occurred in their life is now causing them to stay away from physical activity, thus never understanding the natural effects of the body's process as it relates to exertion.

In this case, we were attempting to present the individual to a good and needed activity. Such activities, so normal for most youth, had turned into something fearful, thus causing the individual to shy away or shut down, when forced into a healthy physical activity. Once the individual realizes they cause these physiological responses at their own will, it is empowering. Knowing that they are creating them internally and understanding how and why, they began to realize they don't have to associate the activity with fear. Through many successful guided experiences and exposure to the activity, the physiological effects become less threatening to the individual. They eventually will acknowledge the experience as beneficial and enjoy the outcome of the activity. They also begin to realize that one can control the physiological effects their body produces. This is a realization all of us need to acknowledge.

Once we do this, we start becoming the powerful being we were created to be. When an individual acknowledges the benefits by doing and processing cause and effect, they lessen the effects of the panic attack when they have one. They realize these are very natural physiological effects, and they can bring them on and shut them off when need be. In so many cases, individuals consciously have no idea what brings on the anxiety and are not even aware of the fact that they are the ones causing the shutting down effect. What a tremendous power to acknowledge that you can experience these effects at your will. We don't always have to associate them with negativity or a traumatic experience.

LIMITING FACTORS

Another example I will share is from the pain clinic. It is a wonderful, eye-opening experience when folks realize there are many ways we can accomplish any number of activities. Sometimes by simple modifications, the activities necessary for us to maintain a standard of living we have become accustomed to can be done again. It becomes a game-changer!

By refocusing our efforts and learning new ways to modify any activity in such a manner so we are not hurting, re-hurting or reinjuring our self. Any activity can be modified. Also, by the selection of another activity from within one's preference domains or other appropriate activity category as long as that does not compromise our body in such a way to cause a pain reaction one can obtain the same desired effects of gratification from the activity involvement.

I would like to add here: *I wish pain on no one.*

"Pain is just pain. It is purposeful, as all things are."

"Its purpose is to let us know something is wrong, physically or emotionally."

"It is neither good nor bad; it is only as we perceive it."

Early in life, I had a prime example of this myself with my father. Long before I was born, being the youngest of ten children, my father worked many jobs to provide for his family. Somewhere along the way, his body gave out and he suffered with back problems throughout his entire adult life. I remember when I was a child, that occasionally there would be weeks at a time, maybe longer, when our father would be home after he would see a chiropractor and doctors in attempts to relieve pain, eventually going back to work.

I recall when I was an early teen, my mother came home from work and sat down with the few of us who were still living at home, in our dining room. She began explaining to us that our Father was in the hospital and needed surgery. She told us the doctors said that with the surgery, they could reasonably assure Dad, that he would be pain-free. However, they could not guarantee that he would not be paralyzed from his waist down due to the risk of surgery in the lower thoracic area. Not knowing much about anything then, I thought those were extreme options. It would be nice for Dad to be pain free!

LIFESTYLE MANAGEMENT

Not so nice to be paralyzed from the waist down. Back in the sixties, surgical techniques were not as specialized as they are now.

The next day, our father was home when I returned from school. I asked him about the surgery and he said "I didn't have it." It was a very short period of time after that, only a few days or probably the following week, when Dad was back to work. A few things changed now. He was working the hoot owl shift. You may be familiar with that term—the midnight shift at the plant. This meant usually there were few workers on duty during this shift. The work was less laborious. The bulk of work was mainly just making sure everything was operating smoothly and would be ready for the morning shift.

Our father loved to play ball and watch sports! Growing up in an orphanage and being placed in foster care, he never had the opportunity to explore his athletic interests. So he took great pleasure in participating when the opportunity arose as an adult. I also noticed that at family functions, Dad's role(s) changed. During the annual baseball games, he now pitched for both teams. He would not attempt to field a ball. He would not go up to bat. He would never leave the pitcher's mound.

I have also remembered seeing him wiping his eyes and hiding his face when I would awake early in the morning, not knowing why nor thinking much of it. I later realized it was because my mother would be out shoveling snow. I realized later, my father knew if he did attempt to help with the shoveling of snow and other certain laborious activity, he would be putting himself in a compromising situation. History taught him that he may end up hurting himself again.

What I had come to realize much later in life was my father made a decision about the necessary modifications he needed to make in his life to live it as effectively and as productively as he could. From the time my father came home from the hospital, I never heard him complain about pain for the rest of his life. He finished his working days, retired as most do, and lived a long life. He had to make some changes and compromises, as we all must do at different times in our life. He did not have the benefit of all the options and alternatives we have today.

LIMITING FACTORS

As one can see, knowledge of what can and will work for us is important to have. With modifications and adaptations that can take place, we can resume almost any activity or replace it with another appropriate activity from our preference domains/areas that will have similar gratifying outcomes.

While we are talking about limiting factors, I will take a moment here to speak of addictions. Addiction of any kind can be problematic when it dictates our actions and behaviors. All disrupt our life's balance, because they command our thoughts. Addictions drive us to unhealthy behaviors and levels of pursuits no matter what the driving force of activity choice or substance. Here we will look at activity itself as the culprit. You have seen in the previous chapters, the benefits of various activity and the statement about being addicted to doing. It takes involvement to experience the benefits of various activities. Some activities stimulate, some relax, some give us sense of accomplishment, euphoric states, gratification etc. These sound good and are, But!

Dang, there *it is again, the Big But!*

— If we feel we always have to be doing something to feel good about ourselves, then something is wrong.
— If we start an activity and find we can't stop, or we dwell on it even when we are not doing it to the detriment of other things that are not getting done, something is wrong.
— If we are losing sleep and wearing ourselves down, something is wrong.

I understand the benefits as well as the destructive qualities of various activities. When we relinquish self-control over our activity choices the activity consumes us and runs our life. Thus instead of being a refreshing, rewarding experience, it becomes another stressor in our life, another limiting factor interfering with our ability to manage our life productively.

We can by reprogramming ourselves, allow ourselves to manage our own life productively and effectively.

Right?

LIFESTYLE MANAGEMENT

Once we have the knowledge and enough successful experiences under our belt and have accomplished the reprogramming process, we are good.

Right?

Once we have the know-how to override psychological and emotional factors, we can manage our life productively.

Right?

I would like to say yes. But here it is again— *The But!*

I mean but.

But what you're probably thinking right about now ...

Well! (That is a deep subject. My spouse would say when I used the term.) So, let's just get to the point!

One must have the resources necessary to follow through what we know is going to work best for us. Resources can represent many things. I consider knowledge a resource. Resources can be time, money, skills, places, equipment, other people, or things.

The fact remains, as I mentioned earlier in chapter 5, most of us have millions of resources available at any moment. We must develop an awareness of them and acknowledge them before we can utilize them when needed. During training sessions when I would focus on resource options available to people, it is fact that any one of us at any given time has four major resource areas to draw from. Those four areas are as follows:

Personal: These are the things that are within us. Our skills, talents, gifts, abilities, our knowledge, our ability to communicate, physical capabilities, and our senses, etc.

Home: These are the things within our home. Our tools, our equipment, appliances, our books, our libraries, our rooms, space, our property, our vehicles. Anything within that which we own and have access to. (Remember the deck of cards.)

Community: These are the things outside the home or property in which we live. Things that we have very easy access to—our neighbors, playgrounds, schools, shopping centers, movie theaters, parks, community services/programs, pools, clubs, organizations, churches, friends, even our workplaces can be resources to us. The list can go on indefinitely.

LIMITING FACTORS

State: These are the things outside of your community. Colleges and universities, government services, parks and historical sites, and natural resources such as rivers, lakes, streams, and mountains. You get the picture!

If the individual or group I am working with at the time have been in a treatment setting, they would have a *fifth* area of resource options. That being the hospital, clinic, or meeting place where we met. For while they were in that program, they had staff, myself, and other participants, as well as a variety of skilled specialists and other options available through that organization.

An exercise I would have them do which took only a few minutes would be what I called a resource awareness exercise. You can do this yourself, on your own, to development your resource inventory and options. I would have them list under each category all the possible options of things to do or use within that particular area. Once they listed all they can think of, I would have each participant, starting with the one that had the shortest list, read their list. Then the next and the next, instructing them as someone reads a resource that they have also but didn't mention on the original list. Add it now to their personal list. By the time the exercise was finished, everyone needs more paper to write all the things down that they and others had identified. By adding the new and additional things they thought of during the process, gives each participant a base awareness of all the resource options they have available, at any given time. Of which they may utilize in time of need.

Once we become aware of the resources that we have at our fingertips, feelings or thoughts of being trapped and not having options or opportunities are lessened. One may find that next time they are in a difficult situation, they can look around and find something that will get them through. Something that can change their outlook in a matter of moments to get them beyond where they are right now. Resources are **things we can do, things we can use, things that we have available** to us. They are the things that we need, to accomplish whatever it is we *need* to do, *want* to do, and *have* to do. I have re-emphasized these three words once again, we will explore in greater detail later on when we look at how we can start developing our own plans of action.

This book is dedicated to present the reader with knowledge and insight into who, what and why we are, and the value of our existence. Knowing and understanding limiting factors that we may experience will better prepare us to compensate for them. All things that can limit us will fall within one of the three Major Limiting Factors.

Knowledge - When we understand our self, how we are created and what makes us unique from everyone else. How we grow and develop. When we understand how things affect us, how to compensate and use what we have and what is available. Once we have the knowledge of self and know how things can affect us, we can get on with our life.

Right? Not So Fast. Just because we have all the knowledge we need, if we don't have the resources to follow through with what we know is going to work for us, we are still stuck.

Resources - When we have all the resources we need (time, skills, money, equipment etc.) we can create the balance we need and get on with our life in a healthy and productive manner.

Right? Well, Not so fast, again. I would like to say yes, but. Dang, those words appear again (Well and Butt), deep and wide subjects.

There is another major limiting factor that tends to shut us down, more often than the other two combined.

Socialization - The fact that we must content with other people in many ways. We will spend much of the of the remaining chapters of this book scratching the surface of how this factor can interfere with managing our life productively.

Chapter 7

Balanced Lifestyle Survey

Now that we have some basic knowledge and understanding of the six involvement areas, or should I say the six classifications of activity, we are ready to determine whether or not we have balance in our life via our involvement in these six areas.

When I am in a treatment setting or a lifestyle management workshop, once we reach this point, I challenge the group to identify any activity that they or someone else can do or imagine doing that would not fall under one of the six involvement areas. Usually, after a few mention certain activities and I, place the activity in the proper category, the group acknowledges: that every activity they identify would fall under one of these six classifications. Upon identifying and reviewing all six activities categories one final time, I challenge the participants to come up with another activity classification. I am always looking and hoping, either by a stroke of genius from somebody or dumb luck, that another activity category will evolve.

I also ask them to identify their strongest and weakest areas of involvement. Once each of them has listed what they think may be their strong and weak areas, I give them the survey.

If the reader would like to take the survey, it is outlined with another exercise after the final chapter of this book.

Instructions: Balanced Lifestyle Survey.

As you know by now, there are millions of activities that can be associated within each category. This survey only identifies ten in

LIFESTYLE MANAGEMENT

each category. You will notice upon reading them, those ten cover a very broad range. Over the years, I would modify and sometimes change the activities, always being careful not to change the basic content of the activity. The replacement would be very similar, but is a more up-to-date version of the activity(s) within those specific categories, hence keeping up with the times and ever-changing and evolving activities in our societies.

You'll notice with each activity, you have three choices. The three choices are *frequently*, *occasionally* and *never*. You must only mark one. You must select one which best describes your involvement in that particular activity. Below, I will describe each:

Frequently: Something you do often. You determine what is frequently. Frequently for some may be once a week (example, going to the gym and working out), whereas others may consider frequently as four or five times a week.

Occasionally: Something you do only every now and then. Once again, you determine what is occasional. This may also be different for everyone (example, going to the movies. I would consider once or twice a year occasional. We have friends who never had children, and they would go to movies almost every evening. They would consider once or twice a week occasional.)

Never: I get to define never. Obviously, never means you have never done it before, *period*. Also, it means that if you have not done the activity at least once in the last year, check never.

Once you have completed the test, count each category separately and score each category separately. For example, in the Creative Expression category, let's say you had three frequently, which are three points each; that would be nine points. You had four occasionally, which are two points each; the total being eight points. You had three checks in the never column, meaning things you have never done or have not done at least once in the last year. These are one point each, making three points. You even get points if you don't do anything at all. Now add the totals: ex. nine plus eight plus three equals twenty points.

Do this for all of the six areas, scoring each separately. Write the score in the space provided for each category. Once you have your six individual scores, you can determine whether you have guessed your strong and weak areas correctly. As to which were your strongest and weakest areas, did you guess yours correctly? If so, you know yourself well!

How do you determine this? Your highest score(s) are your strongest involvement areas. It is these areas of activity where you spend most of your time. Your lowest score(s) are obviously your weakest areas. These are the areas where you may not be getting what you need to maintain a balanced lifestyle. We will explore the effects of not getting what we need from various involvement areas later in this chapter.

You have now established your strongest and weakest areas! One way we can start achieving a more productive balance in our life is by not spending so much time in the areas that we scored exceptionally high. High scores are above twenty-three. We can start devoting some of that time to the areas that we scored exceptionally low in. Low scores are below eighteen.

Keep in mind, if you are comfortable with your lifestyle and it is working for you, no adjustments are necessary. This is just a tool to help identify imbalances when it comes to our involvement.

Now, let's find out where your score(s) compare to the norms. Take all six subtotal scores of each of the categories and add them together. This will give you your final total and score.

Scores below 80: Scoring in this area indicates you are not involved in much of anything. It would be very hard to score this low if you are still alive and are able to think and move. If you are able, have someone check your pulse and resuscitate *you*. I would question whether or not you are still alive. Chances are, you could have died six months ago, and if someone took this test for you, answering on your behalf, you would still have scored over eighty. (Although I have seen a few.)

Scores between 81 and 107: If you score in this range, you are in the retirement or old rocking chair category. It's time to start picking up a little more activity. Selecting activities from areas you scored lowest in would be beneficial. Note, it does not mean the activities have to be one of the few on the survey. There are thousands/millions of options that would fall under the category. If you scored high in any particular category(s), use some of that time to devote specifically to the weakest areas on your survey and you would experience immediate benefit.

Scores between 108 and 135: If you scored in this range, you may very likely have a balanced lifestyle. However in some cases, this is not true. In fact, you may have no balance in your life whatsoever. If you scored exceptionally high in some activity areas and exceptionally low in others, it will place you in the balanced score range. In actuality, there is no balance in your life.

If you scored between eighteen and twenty-three, you are more than likely getting what you need in each of the involvement areas and I wouldn't be too concerned.

Scores between 136 and 155: If you scored in this range, life is good. Or you may be doing too much. It may be time to take a good look at what you are doing and why, and determine if it's meeting your objectives. You may ask yourself some questions. Why are you doing so much? Depending on your answers, you may wish to explore those further. Remember the comment I made earlier? "One can become addicted to activity." Making us feel like we always have to be doing something, it's imperative to keep in mind if and when we are running the activity. Can you stop and start at will with no anxiety or stress, whether or not the task is complete? If so, then we are in control of the activity.

When the activity controls us, we feel that we cannot stop until it is done. We lose sleep, and it's always on our mind even when we are not performing that specific activity. This increases our stress and anxiety, both of which can affect our health, state of mind, and well-being. In these cases, when activities are being selected and done in our leisure, it becomes another chore or another job. This causes a lost opportunity to refresh ourselves physically and intellectually. If you recall from earlier in chapter 4, we have to break up the activity into three major components and in this specific order: *work, chore* and *play*. We cannot neglect any one of these, and must make appropriate and reasonable time for each, allowing us to perform and exist in a healthy manner.

BALANCED LIFESTYLE SURVEY

Scores over 156 and up: Heaven help us! You need to slow down. You are either doing way too much or your perception is way out of the norm. Fortunately, in my career, I've only run into a handful of people who have scored in this range. All of them were in treatment settings for drug and alcohol, crisis unit, or psychiatric facilities. None of them stayed more than four days. They all demonstrated similar symptoms and characteristics. All were intelligent and very inquisitive. I remember them all very vividly; they were that unique. When in a group setting, during a forty-five-minute therapy session, they would have gotten up to go the bathroom at least twice. They would have left the group to get something to drink or a snack at least twice. They were constantly interrupting to ask specific questions. In the moment when you would attempt to answer the first question, they would have asked at least three other questions. For them to stay focused for ten minutes even in private one-on-one sessions was a near impossibility.

How unfortunate for these individuals, so bright, so much to offer, yet unable to stay focused long enough to develop and utilize the skills and gifts they possessed. You usually could spot these folks a mile away, and predict that they would score high on this balanced lifestyle survey. The problem with scoring exceptionally high is we never spend enough time with a particular task to truly get what we need from it. We are always so anxious and ready to move on to something else. So the gratification one gets from completing tasks thoroughly and effectively is virtually nonexistent with these individuals. Just imagine going through life, never experiencing the gratification or the sense of accomplishment that comes from completing a task. That wonderful growth enhancing internal message, *"I'm done"* and *"It's time to move on."* I personally just can't even imagine what that would be like.

I know one of the reasons I still have these vivid memories of those few people. I am sure it is why I choose my profession. I would suspect it's the reason why most therapists who chose to work in treatment settings. We believe we have a calling and a message that will help and benefit others. If we can get that message across to the ones we treat, if they can understand and make sense of it, it can change their life and allow them to experience their gift(s) of life. As a therapist, you always want to help, guide, and make sure everyone gets what they need to get on with their life. These folks, more so than others, leave you with a sense that you have had limited impact, if any. This always leaves an empty space in my heart.

We can only hope, one day?

NOTE: Sometimes results of these exercises when completed accurately, can be very surprising. Results may not always align with our expectations or what appears obvious. You may want someone skilled in their interpretation, review with you. See example(s) below:

An athlete training 8-10 hours a day, may score low in Physical Exercise. This is due to the fact they are spending hours doing sports specific skill development activity to enhance their performance. Remember, there are millions of activities within this category. If we are limiting our involvement to a few. Our score will be low.

This may be fine, although one must use caution, when putting all your eggs into one basket.

This is one of the reasons I like this survey, there is much to be read between the lines, when we look at the whole person. It is where I found imbalance in my life. An artist or musician may score low in Creative Expression. For many of the same reason's sighted above.

You will read another example of many cases, where this tool was beneficial to help see the whole picture along with lack of balance.

About this time during a lifestyle management workshop I would challenge the participants to what I called an *elimination exercise*.

After everyone has scored and reviewed their balanced lifestyle surveys, got the results, and all questions have been answered. I would list the six involvement areas on a screen. I ask them if we had to give up one of the involvement areas, which one would it be? Let's say, we can only have five! Which one would they give up? The groups acknowledging the benefits of each are always very reluctant to give up any, rightfully so. But for the sake of argument, I would tell them something we are all very familiar with. The fact is, we have to *cut back*. We have to get rid of one. Which would it be? I will leave it up to the group, by popular vote—whichever one receives the most votes, that is the one we would eliminate. Once we have a consensus on whichever activity area had the most votes, I would eliminate it from the board or screen. Then, we would discuss what that meant, if we were no longer able to participate in any type of activity associated with that particular activity category. This was always a lot of fun, actually hilarious. After two or three minutes and usually after much debate, the group would agree to get rid of one.

Let's say it is spectator appreciation. I would wipe out the activity area, and then we would discuss what we just gave up. Example, when we give up spectator appreciation, we can no longer spectate or observe. We have the physical ability to reach out and touch, but now we have no sensation of the touch. We can no longer taste, smell, see, or hear. All these are forms of spectation. Imagine if you will:

- Being blind: many people are,
- Being deaf: many people are,
- Not being able to smell: there are some who can't,
- Not being able to taste: there are some who can't, and
- Not being able to feel or have any sensation of touch: some can't.

To remove just one aspect, one component of this activity area from our life would be devastating. Sure, we can live and carry on and adapt if we were missing one or two of the senses. We probably all know somebody in this situation. I don't know of anyone who exists, except in a comatose state of being, that would be considered alive without any ability to spectate or observe in some way, shape, and form.

If any one of us would lose one of the spectative senses, we would have to make some major adjustments in our lifestyle, just to live. When we lose a sense, we learn to rely more effectively on the others, we have to. I've met some remarkable people throughout my life who were blind or deaf individuals who had tremendous hypersensitive awareness of all things around them. They were really remarkable individuals.

LIFESTYLE MANAGEMENT

Well, after losing this one activity category for all intent and purposes, we are still alive. Let's try taking away another one. Once again, I would let the group take a consensus vote. Another activity area would be wiped out. We will explore what it is like no longer being able to participate in any type of activity associated with that activity area. This time, let's say the group decided to take away physical exercise. Now that we can't touch, taste, smell, see, or hear, it would definitely be safer if we were not moving about. Just think about it. If we were able to move about freely, not have any sensory awareness, and we stepped off a 1,000 foot cliff, we would not know it because we would not have the sensation of falling. That is pretty weird to think about, is it not? The really good thing is we would not know when we hit bottom. Even better, we won't feel it when we hit bottom! Think about this, we have no sensory awareness but still have physical capacities. What if everyone is out wandering around? It would have to be aimlessly. What if they would bump into each other? They would not know it or sense it.

We can still think, so maybe we would know, we just can't feel. This is confusing and mind-boggling! What did I just say? We can't hear. Heck, you can't read this. You can't see. This is getting weirder, isn't it? One can only imagine those zombie movies.

Let us take a look at what we actually have lost now. We can no longer move or do physical activities since it no longer exists. We cannot turn our head, lift our arms, nor wiggle a finger or take a step. Fact is, to speak, I must move many body parts. To eat, chew, and swallow require movement. How would I get the food to my mouth? In the group, we could and would go over many scenarios, all of which are hilarious. (I have even been asked if I would do parties!)

Even, getting down to the very basics of movements, such as breathing or our heart beating, this is movement. Without these functions, we would cease to exist in a very short period of time. By now during this exercise, everyone is getting really apprehensive and seriously contemplates what it is they may be giving up, when they are considering any of the remaining four activity involvement areas.

Here we go again. Which one would you give up now, knowing that you can no longer move? Let's say our heart is still beating and we can still keep breathing. I'll let you keep those functions so we can finish the exercise. Also, we have no spectating senses. After much thought and debate and consideration, let's say the group gave up social interaction. What have we lost now? Now, we are all alone. Fact is, we no longer have any physical capacities and no spectator senses. We cannot touch anybody nor taste, smell, see, or hear them. Why bother with them? Now we can't even interact with someone, so what good are they? We might as well get rid of them, although now we have no other means to get our needs taken care of. No one to teach us. No one, period. Our species is going to cease to exist. We are the last; no one will come after us. Pretty gruesome thought, is it not?

Now that we are down to the last three, the apprehension of the group is now becoming great. More curiosity and thought is going into each decision. Where is this all leading?

The group starts thinking about survival mode and what is most valuable to them at this point. Let's say the next one to be voted off would be solitary relaxation. Now, what have we given up? We can't be with other people. Now we can't be alone. This is starting to seem like a *Twilight Zone* episode. What have we lost? Now we can no longer rest, sleep, rejuvenate, recuperate, and relax. Wait a minute. We can't move, so how can we not relax?

What the!

Needless to say, without rest or sleep, we cannot exist very long. Have you ever gone one night without sleeping?

We all have pulled all-nighters studying or traveling one time or another. Sleep and sleep patterns are an interesting topic. I have come to many theories and conclusions on reasons for insomnia, sleep behaviors, and requirements in various stages of our life. I will not explore in this book, other than stating sleep is vital to our health and well-being. I will say that an interesting phenomenon takes place when we are sleep-deprived. We get a false sense of elation and energy in some cases. I recall the one time I intentionally stayed up all night. It was back in my college days, studying for an exam that I had first thing in the morning. After the final exam was over, I felt great! I knew I was going to crash, but since I felt so good now, I decided I

LIFESTYLE MANAGEMENT

would go to the gym to get my workout in, and then crash. I realized after my first exercise my efficiency was way below the norm, even though I felt great and energized. After the second exercise experiencing the same subpar performance, I decided I'd better rest to avoid continued frustration and inefficiency.

I have had many patients over the years tell me that they do better when they were sleep-deprived. My comment to them is, you just think you do. I challenge them to test themselves with tasks that involve and require great physical or concentration ability and you'll soon find you are nowhere near the peak performance. We always look for justifications for our choices, good or bad.

Where were we? Down to our last two. Creative expression or intellectual stimulation. Which one will it be?

At this point, the group may select intellectual stimulation because they don't want to think about it anymore. What would life be without thought? Hell if I know. I can't think anymore. That was just taken away. Well, let me tell you, this may be one of the reasons that led me into this profession. Remember the questions I was asked at a young age that I shared with you earlier in this book?

Here's one I forgot to mention, *"Don't you ever think before you act?"*

I heard that a lot, also. There you have it. We can't think any longer. Heck, who wants to at this point? We are just there. We don't know it, though, because we can't think and can't process. We don't even know if we are imagining this whole ordeal. Just imagine what that would be like. Oops, we can't! Fact is, who cares? Fact is, no one. Fact is, we don't know if anyone does. Fact is, we have no capacity to acknowledge whether we care.

That leaves us with one—the creative expression category of activity. When that is gone, we have nothing new; no new actions which we can't perform, anyhow. No new thoughts which we can't think, anyhow, at this point. Fact is, I don't know where we go from here as I can no longer think. That's already gone.

Yet with creativity, there is always hope! As long as there is creativity, something can happen, I just don't know how. I no longer, at present, have that capacity when the last activity category was removed. It's always interesting to explore what life would be like without any creativity from the beginning of time. Let us explore for moment.

What if no one invented the wheel? What would life be like?

What if cars were never invented? What would life be like?

What if no one decided to get under a tree, go into a cave or seek shelter from the elements? What would life be like?

What if construction and design never took place? What would life be like?

What if no one decided to plant the seed? What would life be like?

What if no one picked up a stone and threw it and downed game to eat? What would life be like?

What if there were no grocery stores? What would life be like?

What if no one cooked over fire? What would life be like?

What if instruments were never invented? What would life be like?

What if no one took colorful elements and placed them on a backing/canvas no art? What would life be like?

Without creativity, life looks pretty dismal. Who knows? As long as there is creativity, we may be able to figure a way out of this mess, we have gotten ourselves into, with this exercise. That would take a creative process!

Ending this chapter with a philosophic note:

It may have been creativity that brought us into this world. It was certainly creativity which has allowed us to advance and exist within this world. It may be the very last experience we have as we leave this world. I have never died before. That will be a new experience. It is my hope and belief, we will experience a new creation when that time comes.

Chapter 8

Why We Do the Things We Do?

In this chapter, we will explore benefits from activity, along with an explanation of preference domain areas. There are many reasons why people do specific things; some good, some not so good. We can spend hours discussing why one would do this or that. We may have asked ourselves that very question many a time.

During my lifestyle management courses, when we get to this point, I would ask everyone the question, *"Have you ever asked yourself why you do the things you do?"*

The answer I usually get from many in the program is this, *"I ask myself that all the time."*

Occasionally, I would get another response that is also very common, *"My spouse does all the time."* Usually, after the fact, someone would ask, *"Why the hell did you do that?"*

The next question I ask is, *"Do you ever get any good answers?"* The answer is usually *"No"* or *"Not as of yet!"*

After a good laugh, once people share some examples and experiences, we do some exploring and find there are many legitimate reasons why people do the things they do. Then, I start compiling a list on a chalkboard, flip chart, overhead projector (I'm really dating myself at this point), or video screen, computer, or tablet image or whichever medium was being provided at the time. What would begin to emerge is what we refer to as *major motivators.*

Let us explore these major motivators. These are the things which most of us hope to achieve from the activities we participate in whether it is though our work, chores, or play/recreation activity. Researchers determined that there are *ten major motivators.* Meaning, these were the most frequent responses that came up when people had been surveyed and asked to identify why they do certain activities, along with what benefits they hope to obtain by participating in them. Let's run through them, and I will briefly describe what each entails:

Ten major motivators:

Relaxation: to rest, unwind, sleep, and regroup.

Enjoyment: to do things just because we enjoy doing them. Nothing expected, except a pleasant and pleasurable experience.

Fitness: to perform any activity that will enhance our physical being and conditioning level.

Sense of accomplishment: activities engaged in to allow us to accomplish things or to get things done.

Socialization: being and interacting with other people.

Being helpful: doing activities to be of benefit to someone else.

Filling time: activities we involve ourselves in that have no real outcome other than being done to keep busy and pass the time; nothing expected, nothing intended.

Excitement: activities that stimulate and excite you; this is different for everyone. Some may find rock-climbing, skydiving, or white-water rafting exciting; others may find reading a new book or going out to dinner exciting.

Freedom: activities that enhance your sense of freedom and/or independence.

Creativity: activity that taps into our creative juices allowing us to explore and getting us out of the routine and into new and different things; doing things we have never done before.

These are the ten major motivators. I like to refer to them as our intrinsic motivators because they are inherent to us and our personality, our very makeup. When our lifestyle is designed in such a manner that it's gratifying whatever our personal major motivators may be, life is good. When the activities we choose do not align with nor gratify whatever our major motivators may be, then life is not so good. It doesn't matter where and how we gratify our major motivators, whether in the workplace, at home, or in the communities, or how regularly. Although, it must be frequent enough to keep us physically and intellectually refreshed.

If it can be accomplished in the workplace, how ideal. If this is the case, our jobs will truly be a pleasure. We kill two birds with one stone, so to speak. For many of us, unfortunately, that may not be the case. So we must be selective about how we spend our time. Let me also say, guard our time to make sure we are incorporating the right types of task and activity that will allow us to gratify our intrinsic motivators. If it can be done at home through our chores, for some if that be the case, it is another plus. Once again, I'll have to mention that it doesn't work for most of us in either of those two areas. So what most of us have to do at proper intervals throughout the year, during our vacations, or time off, is go places and do things that will gratify our major motivators. This will help keep us refreshed and satisfied, along with assisting in maintaining balance to keep ourselves moving forward productively in life.

What I tend to see way to often with people seeking my services is just the opposite. People whose lifestyle does not in any way, shape, or form align in any reasonable manner of which to gratify their personal major motivators.

In the treatment centers where I have worked and had lifestyle management education programs, I have found nearly 100%, if not all, of my patients and individuals seeking my assistance were involved in activities that did not align with their motivators. The actual activities they were involved in aligned with their absolute lowest responses on the *group benefit exercise* which identifies one's major motivators.

When studying the statistical data and interviewing patients and individuals seeking assistance to manage their life more effectively, I have found this conclusion to be true. When our life's involvement is not aligned with our personal major motivators, our symptomatology can and usually does increase significantly. Even with healthy individuals, when someone has a limiting condition such as prolonged illness or injury, it magnifies the other symptoms they may already be experiencing.

Let me explain using the following example to put things in perspective. An individual with a psychiatric diagnosis comes to treatment, participates in the program, and is learning what he must. He says the right things, gets his medicines adjusted properly, sleeps properly, and eats nutritiously. While he is in the hospital, he recovers to a fairly normal, or at least a stable, level of functioning. He leaves treatment, makes no adjustments in his lifestyle, nor in his choice of activities.

In the long run, this individual will be seeking treatment again in the not too distant future. Many return to the same situation, same circumstances, and get involved in the same activities as they have done before. They will make no adjustments despite what they have learned, other than a possible change of their prescription. I have seen this happen over and over again upon patients returning to treatment. These are some of the comments I have received from people in this circumstance during interviews. When asked about their involvement and how they felt when performing activities they have identified, none of which aligned with their personal major motivators, some of their comments are summarized in the next paragraph.

They identify feeling (symptoms) of emptiness, loneliness, lack of personal gratification, feeling useless, worthless, depressed, increased stress levels, increased anxiety, anger, frustration, boredom, no sense of direction, no fulfillment, increased tension, sleeplessness, increased blood pressure, more frequent headaches. It goes on and on and on. Just reading this list makes me feel miserable. Try it yourself, just focus on the comments listed above. See what I mean?

I'm assuming, if you're reading this book, you are a pretty healthy individual, and like many of us, always want to improve yourself and your purpose of existence. Hopefully for the most part, you are gratifying your major motivators consistently and you are comfortable with your lifestyle. If you are looking at that list, thinking, *By gosh, I experience some or all of those things, way too regularly,* either way, I'm glad you are reading this book. Understanding our makeup and our personal motivators will be beneficial when selecting and incorporating activity options into our life.

I sincerely hope it gives you a starting point to manage your life more effectively, if need be. We will all face things in our life which will require major changes in our lifestyle, whether it be good, bad, or just typical circumstances.

Let's take a look at the good ones first—promotions which may require us to relocate, marriage, or the birth of a child. Some bad ones, such as injury; illness whether it be physical, psychological, social, emotional, or spiritual; loss of a job; or natural disasters.

Things such as graduations, military service, having to care for an elderly loved one, or having to work an extra job to make ends meet. These are typical circumstances that may require big adjustments in our lifestyle. All of these things disrupt and require changes in our lifestyle. Some are temporary, others long-term—all can prevent or hinder our ability to gratify our own needs.

When we understand ourselves and our own makeup better, the whole process of creating balance in our life becomes easier. Aligning our involvement to gratify our intrinsic needs makes the transitions more comfortable. When we don't understand our unique makeup, it will not matter how much time or money we spend or what we do. We will continue to experience many of the same outcomes and symptoms.

Yes, we may improve our skills and accomplish many wonderful things. We may receive many accolades for our achievements which may still leave us feeling empty. I would like to share an experience I had with a patient at this point. An individual I had the opportunity to work with, who was in a psychiatric facility. After reviewing his case records, this late twenties male with an excellent paying job, great family background, apparently happily married, with two children. He was a tennis player and golfer ranking in the top three by the state amateur ranking system the past three years. Without getting into any further detail, looking at his profile, I wished I had his lifestyle. Upon interviewing him, I am hearing from him a lot of the symptomatology mentioned above. We decided to do some more exploring.

WHY WE DO THE THINGS WE DO?

The patient was a smart, intelligent, athletic, handsome individual. He had a great job and a good family. At this point I'm thinking, I would have traded him Even/Steven—his lifestyle for mine. In everything except family, of course. I definitely would have gotten the better deal! Though, he was no fool! The evaluation testing was completed, tabulated, and scored, and the results reviewed with the patient. The educational process began.

It soon became apparent, the reasons for the symptoms he experienced, which had led him to seek treatment, were due to the fact that he had not made appropriate changes when needed in his activity involvement. What appeared apparent to him initially and what was seemingly an easy fix did not work for this individual. What we found was other than his work environment, he was focusing all his energy on the two things he was exceptionally good at—his golf and tennis games.

He had reached the point in his life that many of us do. Let me correct that. Actually, all of us will reach eventually at some point in our lives. What happens is we reach our productive years, usually in our early to mid-twenties, and actually today is more toward our late twenties and early thirties. At this point, another major change occurs in our life when we reach this stage. From the time we reach our middle/late teens, we are entering into the specialization stage of our natural play development and evolution. During this stage, we will start to select specific activities which we are exceptionally good at or want to be exceptionally good at. If we are athletic, we will pick one or two sports where we really want to focus our energies and efforts. If we are very creative, we will select specific ways to specialize that creativity, whether it is through our interest in art, drama, music, dance, etc. If we are very social, we have our clique of friends. We may get involved with councils at school, social clubs, our churches, etc. If our forte happens to be in the spectator realm, we will be in the cheering sections and be at the pep rallies. We will be going to the concerts, etc. Once we are in our early twenties, maybe we are starting our careers or in college and our time is limited. We have other duties and responsibilities we must fulfill. Due to time constraints, we become more selective as to the activities we wish to be involved in. Since our time is limited, we tend to focus on the one or two activities from our specialization stage that we were exceptionally good at, and we stick with those. We do so because they are still fun. We are good at them. We don't have to spend or invest a lot of time developing the required skill set, which is a plus at this point in our life because now we are working, raising our families, and maintaining our property. We don't have large chunks of time and rarely take the time to develop new skills. We can just enjoy the participation and the experience that goes along with the activity(s) we are good at. Also, the connection and camaraderie the activity may offer is still working for us to a point. We know this from past experience for we've been involved in these activities for the last ten to twelve years.

What I have seen so often in my work is that we will stick with activities for so long because of these very facts. We tend to stick with those activities we were exceptionally good at in our late teens or early twenties for the next twenty, thirty, or forty years. In many cases, throughout our entire productive stage of our development, time and routine are the culprit. During our careers, the average productive adult—one who was working and raising a family—may have anywhere between an hour and a half to three hours of leisure on a typical day. That is not always one block of time. It may be fifteen minutes here, twenty minutes there, or half an hour here, this time may be divvied up between our jobs, community responsibilities, home, and family responsibilities. We simply do not have the free time we once had. The time that is necessary to devote to developing new specific skills in order to learn and master a new activity(s). So we stick with those one or two activities we once enjoyed and were good at until we wear them right into the ground.

I've heard some of these following phrases many times throughout my career. I've had ladies tell me, "I've quilted quilts for everyone in the family" "I used to love quilting" "In fact, I've got three of them in the closet that I've been working on and need to finish. It's been three years, and I can't even force myself to get them down."

I can't even count the number of men that I've heard say, "I used to love to play golf" "I would play at the drop of a hat. I keep clubs in the trunk of my car, and so if an opportunity came up, I was ready right now, man."

Some would say, "I keep my favorite clubs in the back seat of my car. It's been seven years and I haven't got them out yet" "I have no interest in playing again."

It may sound like I am picking on the golfers here. I also had many say, "Last time I played was four years ago after playing for thirty-five years three or four times a week. I used to be good. Now I get so frustrated. The last time I played, I just threw my clubs in the water trap and haven't played since."

The point I want to make is, during our productive years, because of lack of time to explore, we stick with the activities we were exceptionally good at for the reasons mentioned until they no longer work for us. We may have long since lost the skill, or should I say level of play, we once had due to age or condition. We have just worn out the activity(s).

We should always keep in mind any activity in the novelty stage is when it is most productive for us. Especially when it comes to refreshing us physically and intellectually, and when we are *learning* and developing the skills, no matter what our age. Novelty, meaning when the activities are new. This is when the activity is most intriguing, challenging, and exciting. We get more benefits from the involvement due to this fact. "More bang for the buck"!

Reiterating what I mentioned earlier in this book, when we are learning things we have never done before, we have no reference memory physically for our musculature or mentally, as to how to do the skill(s). We learn them no matter what age, condition, or physical functional capacity required of the activity with the skills we bring to the table. At whatever stage in life we happen to be in at that time, the learning is taking place. For many, instead of picking up new activities along the way that will meet our needs at this point, stage, condition, or functional capability in our life, we don't. Many injure themselves attempting to maintain previous levels of participation in the activity they once excelled in. We may end up not doing anything for fear, lack of time, or having no idea what it is that would interest us in our current stage of life or age.

LIFESTYLE MANAGEMENT

Another self-defeating comment I also hear so often, which becomes an issue with many of our older population—the fifty plus group—is this: "I've done everything."

Not!

That always makes me laugh every time I hear that. My response is, *"You're not even close!"*

So where is all this leading with this young male patient? Upon reviewing the evaluation results, it was apparent that his activity did not align with his preference domains. Preference domains are activity areas that we score high in. We know two things about our Preference Domains, not to be confused with categories of activity, these are identified from more extensive testing.

Number one: Our potential to excel and do well at almost any activity within our preference domain areas is tremendous if we allow ourselves ample opportunity. This means allowing yourself enough time to participate in the activity to develop the skills necessary to perform it well and experiencing it regularly.

Number two: Our preference domains are the things that work best for us to refresh us physically and intellectually.

This makes me think of the actual definition and essence of the word *recreation,* which is, to re-create, make anew, refreshment of mind and body through diverting activity.

It is nothing more than an experience!

What this patient explained to me when we explored this information, was that he thought if he devoted even more time to the things he was already exceptionally good at, in this case his golf and tennis games, and if he continued to develop his skills and improve his game, this would make him feel better. He explained that the more he trained and the more he worked on fine tuning his skills and improving his games(s), the less satisfied he felt.

He kept thinking, "As I get better, when I become number one in the state, that will gratify me and I will feel better about myself and who I am."

In the process, he spent less time with his wife and children, even though he knew and felt this is what he needed to be doing, especially at this time in his life. He felt more empty and more isolated. He explained it became a vicious cycle, feeling that if he would accomplish this one thing, reach this goal—the number one ranking or title in one or the other or both sports—if he could reach this goal, then things would be better. "Alas, it wasn't working, and here I am."

Early on in treatment during the educational program, he began to learn more about himself. With the help of some of the self-exploratory exercises and discussions during the lifestyle management process he started to become aware of a few things. He realized that not only was his activity not aligning with his preference domains, his choice of activities was not gratifying his intrinsic motivators—his major motivators.

If you recall some of the symptomatology we expressed earlier, when this mal-alignment occurs. Imagine this young man with great skills, great career, and financially set, which many at first glance would view as the ideal lifestyle. He was not happy, not content. In fact, he was making his own life miserable, despite all the blessings he had around him at the time. I also experienced this at one point in my life in college. The classic case of letting an activity(s) direct and run our life. Another aspect of his lifestyle that became apparent was the fact that he was meeting very few of his social needs, especially the ones that were dearest and most important to him.

We will explore *basic social needs* in the upcoming chapters. At the end of this book, there is also an exercise called the *group benefit exercise* which will identify one's major motivators. Generally, I do not like to give forced choice tests or questionnaires for the simple fact that they are limiting and pigeonhole one's responses. However, with this exercise, I believe it is imperative we make a decision even when we may appear to like or dislike the two choices. As you will see, what this exercise does is force you to compare one against the other. It forces you to make a choice! We cannot be wishy-washy when it comes to determining who we really are. These tests only take a few minutes to complete and score. This is one of the reasons I like it. Not to mention that if the person taking the test truly answers honestly, it's very accurate. After taking the group benefit exercise, you will know why you do the things you do. Or should I more accurately say, why we should be doing the things that we do?

LIFESTYLE MANAGEMENT

There is a question I'm frequently asked, which I am sure many of you will be asking when taking this test yourself. Which is, "I like both equally, which should I chose?" I will then always ask them, "What do you like about them?" or "Why do you dislike them?" Their answer is usually identified in their responses.

For example, someone may have difficulty deciding between, the *enjoyment* benefit versus the *fitness* benefit. A simple question from me being, "Why is this a dilemma?" Elicits a response very similar to this: "I need to exercise, I recognize the benefit, and I just *enjoy* doing it." They just answered their own questions. *Enjoyment!*

Another example of decision difficulty can be between *sense of accomplishment* and *being helpful*. "I like them both equally." Once again, with a simple question or two such as, "Why is it you like a sense of accomplishment?" The response: "I like getting things *done*." Same question for being helpful, and the typical response is, "When I do things for other people, it makes me feel good." "Why?" I ask. "I want to *help* them." As you see, your responses to the questions will lead you to your answer, (which come from within).

If there is still an indecision, then I may ask something similar to this. "How would you rather help somebody"? Give them one hundred dollars or assist them with the project that will improve their home If the individual chooses to assist with the home improvement, it is more than likely they like to see *accomplishments* for their efforts.

Keep in mind, the most common reason why people score high in sense of accomplishment is they simply like to accomplish things and to get things done. It's the same case with dislikes.

For example, someone may have a difficult time deciding between *relaxation* and *filling* time. "Which one should I choose when I dislike both equally?" My question to them is, "Why do you dislike relaxation?" Response: "It's a waste of time."

My next question, "What's the problem with filling time?" Here I usually reiterate the definition we covered during the educational session leading up to the exercise describing *filling* time—doing things just to pass the time; nothing expected nothing intended. If there is still a question, I will remind them of the basic behaviors such as sleep, recuperation, and acknowledging relaxation/sleep which are necessary processes for maintaining health. Also I mention it is one of the six involvement areas which is necessary for maintaining balance when used effectively. By now, they have already made the choice. They may choose *relaxation* if they were concerned about productive time use. They may choose *filling time* if it's more important that they keep their time occupied to allow distractions if they have trouble controlling thoughts.

Instructions for taking the group benefit exercise to identify your major motivators is included with that test at the end of this book.

You may want to stop now for a few minutes to complete the test. Once completed and scored, resume this chapter and ask yourself some of the following questions:

1. Are the things that I do in my life gratifying my top three responses in some way, either through my work, chore, or leisure pursuits? If they are, you're probably pretty comfortable with your lifestyle, and it's probably working very well for you.
2. If not, why? My guess is if you examine the types of things you are doing most often, they more than likely are not aligning with your major motivators. Remember what we explained earlier in this chapter describing some of the symptoms people experience. Even with a healthy group of individuals, when their involvement does not align or gear to the gratification of their major motivators (top three responses), they may experience many of the symptoms. The affects may not be devastating enough to be hospitalized, seek assistance or treatment, although they may experience lack of personal gratification and boredom. What I hear often is, "I just get frustrated" or "I don't know what else to do." There is an emptiness in their lives caused by their choice of activity.

LIFESTYLE MANAGEMENT

When we realize that our activity does not align with our major motivators and we can make adjustments, it is usually a pleasant surprise. Knowing just by selecting activities that will gratify our major motivators, we can make a huge difference in our life when it comes to feeling more content and productive by what we are doing.

This process is kind of fun, isn't it?

Let's face it. What better subject to study, understand, and know inside and out and be the expert on than you? You are a fascinating subject! You will begin to realize how fascinating and interesting you really are as you continue through this process. If you can recall from chapter 3, the remarkable creature our Lord created is *man*—that's us!

In our unique form and design, we have an unbelievable ability to adjust and adapt to circumstances, situations, and extremes. We live on every continent in the world and in some of the harshest conditions. It is always so important to keep an open mind to our needs and the needs of others. Be open to the guidance of our Creator. The reason we are here is to succeed and fulfill our destiny. I'm reminded of a quote (chapter 7, verse 15–17, as well as the whole chapter of the Book of Wisdom in the Catholic Bible), "For he is the guide of wisdom and the director of the wise. Both we and our words are in his hand, as well as all prudence and knowledge." Also, chapter 16, verses 1–3 in the Gospel according to Matthew in the King James and Catholic Bibles. To paraphrase this scripture, "In our foolishness, we are able to read signs of the season, but do not always recognize the signs within us. Even more so, not recognizing nor interpreting the signs our Creator, has placed within each of us."

We need to be able to read ourselves to be able to recognize those internal messages. We need to be able to interpret our own instincts/guardian angel/subconscious which are only designed to protect us.

Chapter 9

Components of Self

After those last few chapters, you're beginning to understand more about yourself. What makes each one of us so unique and the complex creatures that we are. You now know your strongest areas of involvement. You also now know your intrinsic motivators. You understand there are many limiting factors that can interfere with managing your life effectively, as well as resource areas we can draw upon to assist in the process.

Next, we will begin to take a look at each component and entity that makes up each one of us. Each individual has five separate components whether we realize it or not. It is these entities that make each one of us unique and complex. These five components are our physical being, intellectual being, emotional being, social, and spiritual beings.

An interesting thing about the human makeup is that each component is a unique and separate entity within us. As we acknowledge and understand individual components, we can allow them to develop, grow, or shall I say evolve. Evolve is what they truly do when the developmental process is not disrupted. I don't know whether to say it is fortunate or unfortunate that each may develop separately. They can also cease to develop separately from one another. I will explain this process throughout this chapter.

First, let's take a look at each component separately. We will start with the most obvious.

LIFESTYLE MANAGEMENT

First, the physical component: For apparent reasons, this is the most obvious. This is what we see when we look in the mirror. This is what other people see when they look at us. As mentioned earlier in this book, the body develops at its own pace. Of course, with some fluctuation in age, usually within a few years, depending on our body type, nutrition, and our developmental stages. I think all will agree that, by the time we reach our mid-twenties, our bodies reach their maximal growth, except for the few outliers where natural growth may continue or be affected by other things. This growth process will mature at its own rate naturally if the body is fed properly. Not much is going to interfere with this process.

Second, the intellectual component: For apparent reasons, this is the next most obvious component of self. We don't always see it or acknowledge it when we see the individual, although usually we can determine to some degree once an individual speaks. I know I'm being way too general here with that statement. It is our communication with one another that may help us predict the level of education or intelligence of an individual. Of course, by testing, we can determine one's IQ level. There's not much that interferes with the intellectual development, except, of course, any developmental condition, illness, accidents where one sustains a brain injury, substance abuse, or for whatever reason we choose not to learn and develop our cognitive skills. Our intellect will continue to develop as we learn, as we experience new things, and hopefully grow wiser as years pass.

Third, the emotional component of self: Now here is an interesting character of each individual. Are emotions not the effect of some sort of physiologic state, bought on or caused by a thought process? Aha, well yes. Let's explore emotions and purpose. There is a vast array of emotions/feelings.

Can we label all the emotions?

There are many emotions that we experience throughout the day, and there are various degrees of each emotion. Examples: happy, delighted, excited, or upset, angry, furious. Another example: sad, hurt, miserable, devastated. As you can see, these are just a few examples of emotions that we can put into words and the varying degrees of each. I don't know about you, but at times, there just doesn't seem to be a word to explain or match a particular emotion I may be experiencing. To put a label on what you are experiencing in certain situations or circumstances can be very difficult. Yes, so many emotions! How do we recognize, label, and express them?

It has always been my belief that we are in control of our emotions. Also, that each emotion is purposeful and jam-packed full of energy. When we know this and accept it and learn how to recognize and interpret them, then we will be able to use them and their energy effectively. By being able to recognize the proper emotion, we are experiencing we can welcome the energy it provokes. We can then use that energy to resolve conflicts or issues we are being faced with.

I understand this is not an easy thing for many to accept. With each new program, with each new training session, I have to convince many of this fact. When working with a healthy population not associated with a treatment setting, this is not too difficult to accomplish. On the other hand, performing a lifestyle management education program for an unhealthy population, whether in a pain clinic, psychiatric facility, crisis unit, partial hospitalization, or drug and alcohol treatment centers, this is much more difficult to accomplish. Only by experiencing multiple specifically designed activities to provoke certain emotions within us and by active participation can the participants begin to understand and make the connection.

During workshops and treatment training programs when we are discussing emotions, I like to have the participants identify emotions, to see how many we can come up with. I will list them on a screen for all to see. Then after filling a screen with numerous emotions identified by the group, and everyone acknowledges that there are various degrees of each, I like to ask them a question.

What is the purpose of emotion? There are many emotions, they serve but one purpose. That purpose being to provide us with the stimulation, that energy to do whatever is necessary to be done in that situation. Plain and simple. The purpose of all emotion is to *provoke action*. That's it! Tons of emotions; all but for one purpose.

I also like to explore with each group this question: Who controls your emotions?

LIFESTYLE MANAGEMENT

This always leads to some interesting debate. Some will acknowledge they control their emotions, but (there is that big *but* again) ... I will, at this time, get several examples from the group. One very common one is, "My husband just makes me so mad" or "My daughter makes me furious."

We will listen to several people who give me examples of how other people make them feel whatever they are feeling at that particular moment. We then review the set of circumstances, causing the emotional reaction within them. I then ask this next question: "Where do your emotions come from?"

Other than an occasional, "I don't know," the group acknowledges that emotions come from within each one of us. The emotion we experience is triggered by the brain consciously and sometimes subconsciously reacting to a certain medium or situation. It is always very surprising to me that there are so many people who feel they have no control over their emotions, though I can understand why. Emotions are very powerful things. They are the greatest force within us; the most powerful force known to the human race. Emotions can raise us to such great heights where we can accomplish anything we set out to do. Emotions can devastate us to such terrible lows that we are willing to hurt ourselves or others. Nothing in life has that kind of power.

We talked about hysterical strength in an earlier chapter brought on by a rush of adrenaline which is provoked and produced by one's emotions. So, we have this wonderful power within each of us at our fingertips. Isn't that amazing?

For someone who has not already known this or accepted this fact, it is an amazing awakening, acknowledging that they have been given this very powerful tool—one of the most wonderful features of our design. So why don't we use it? It would certainly make life easy.

Here are a few of the things I found to be pretty consistent in all of our lives in reference to emotion:

1. *Emotions are powerful things.* The first time we may experience a certain situation that provokes a particular emotion, although powerful, we are capable of harnessing that power if we use it

effectively. What happens when we don't use it effectively? Next time we are in a similar situation that provokes this particular emotion, our subconscious realizes that last time enough energy wasn't produced to provoke the correct action. So what do you think the body and brain's response is?

You guessed it. It produces even more energy in hopes to provoke enough action to solve or resolve what's causing this emotion to kick in. If the individual continues to shut down each time this occurs, more and more energy is produced. Thus, bringing on such a rush of emotional energy, one becomes overwhelmed with this tremendous force they feel building up within them. With each failure to express and/or utilize the energy productively comes an even greater sense of lack of control or hopelessness within the individual. I am sure this can be very scary—a sense of having absolutely no control over this force inside of them provoked by their emotions. I can see how this can cause one to panic when they experience the energy and effects of the physiology. The essence of our potential and true strength.

I could share numerous experiences I have had throughout my and others' athletic careers; people who have learned to control and use their emotions. Those who could bring about the force from the emotion at the very instant it is needed to accomplish what no one else had before them. Let me point out to those reading this, controlling emotion is not suppression of them, but recognizing and utilizing them effectively.

2. *Sometimes they are hard to identify.* There are many! It is so important to be able to recognize the correct emotion before we can express it effectively. Many in our older generation have been taught not to express emotion. Of course, this has changed. Actually, the opposite may be true today with people expressing anything, anywhere, without care or concern for anyone else. Although, my guess is what they are expressing and identifying is not the correct emotion, either.

I will give a personal example. Early in my young adult life, I liked to think I was invincible. I could do anything I needed

LIFESTYLE MANAGEMENT

to do myself. When faced with situations that I either didn't have the knowledge, the skill, or equipment, I found myself very angry. Whenever faced with something I really didn't have control over, I got angry. Because of my strength and aggression, people would have to deal with my anger. The problem was, I never resolved the problem. Anger wasn't the issue. Once I realized why I was getting so angry under certain circumstances after exploring the situation, the fact was the realization that there were certain things I could not do or could not do on my own. I needed help!

The problem was, I wasn't used to asking for help, nor anywhere in my makeup was there any acknowledgment that there was something I could not do. This sense of *helplessness* I experienced in certain situations caused thoughts of frustration provoking anger within me.

So it wasn't anger, although this is what I had interpreted and let surface, that I had control over. Anger, to me, was acceptable, helplessness was not. What I didn't have control of because I never experienced it before, was helplessness. Or I should say I would not let myself acknowledge it at the time. Helplessness was a hard one for me to accept. Once I acknowledged that and accepted it, I realized and learned it was OK to ask for help with what I needed. I saved myself and others around me a lot of grief. The bonus along with it was I was getting my needs met effectively. You know what? That brought me closer to people around me—family and friends. Another bonus!

3. *Expressing them can be very problematic.* When we experience some of the physiological symptoms that we explored with the example in chapter 7; the individual who had a panic disorder and the physical exercise exposure treatment sessions (Panic, isn't that an emotion?). Let me answer that, this way. Panic is a state of mind, that may provoke certain emotions. Which in turn may set into motion a variety of physiologic responses.

I'm sure we have all tried to express an emotion when we were nervous. Our heart rate was up, and had a giant lump in our throat. It is just very difficult to get our point across under those circumstances. Sometimes because of the anxiety, as we experienced in that one case, the emotion shuts us down.

4. *We mask them.* Many of us may not be honest with our emotions for whatever reason. My guess is either fear or deceit. Either way, it's disruptive and can be destructive to ourselves and others when the true emotions are not expressed effectively, for in those cases, neither party is going to get their needs met, and external or internal issues will not get resolved.

So please keep in mind, for I cannot re-emphasize nor re-enforce this enough, emotions are a very powerful thing. They can raise us to great heights so we can accomplish anything we set out to do or devastate us to such terrible lows that we are willing to hurt ourselves or others. There is no greater force known to the human race. We all possess this power. It is within us. It is ours to control and to use at will.

As mentioned it has always been my belief we are in control of our emotions. Each is purposeful and full of energy. When we know this and can learn to interpret the proper emotion that we are experiencing and what is provoking it, we can use the energy from it to resolve the conflict or issues we are faced with that provoked it. I acknowledge for many this is a tough one to swallow, for with it we must become responsible. I have mentioned how difficult this can be for some people.

With each new program and with each new training session, I have to convince many of this fact. For those individuals who allow themselves to be shut down time and time again, it is like driving a six-inch spike into a seasoned oak plank with your thumb to get them to accept this. They do not want to accept the fact that they produce and can control their own emotions. Along with the fact they are responsible for them, and the action(s) they chose when they experience them. Once this painstaking process is complete, it will only be acknowledged, absorbed, and accepted when the participants have had an opportunity to experience it. Proof is in the pudding, so to speak!

LIFESTYLE MANAGEMENT

One must experience and be able to match the emotion with the action, activity, or cause that had provoked it, of course. These successful experiences help bring home this fact and awareness. When they can experience this at will and repeatedly, they begin to understand. Yes, this power is within them. They can experience it, and turn it on and off as needed.

As the instructor or therapist, I can introduce an exercise(s) at this point; an activity which will provoke particular emotions. After the exercise, you can focus on exploring what emotion(s) surfaced and whether it was correct for the situation.

At that point, I would use another activity to allow participants to experience an opposite emotional reaction. Only then after experiencing the emotion and what provoked it and the ability to change what we feel all within the matter of minutes during the same session and same environment do we then begin to understand and accept the fact that we do and can control our emotions within good, bad, or indifferent situations.

With that comes an amazing awakening and acknowledgment of a very powerful tool we have been given. With this acceptance and knowledge, they are being empowered!

Easy, right?

Unfortunately, I am amazed how often, I run into people who for whatever reason do not acknowledge this fact. There are those who, not only don't accept that they can control and manipulate their emotions. They put the cause and blame in the hands of others. Thus, attempting to place the power they possess, into the hands of someone else. This of course is impossible. But, (again, with the buts) if one perceives and believes someone else controls their feelings/emotions, they are in Big Trouble. This puts them in a peculiar predicament, where they place themselves under the influence of others. This puts them in situations where they can be easily manipulated. Thus gratifying needs of others in hopes to fulfill their own. When in fact, all this does is get them further and further from meeting their own and filling their purpose and destiny. Remember the comment in the first chapter of this book, you are a complete package with amazing tools and abilities, just waiting to be recognized and developed. They are being empowered! Easy, right?

Emotions are one of our greatest tools, one of the most wonderful features of our design that we squander by not acknowledging it. My wish is that each and every one of the readers, actually each and every one of the human race, would acknowledge this fact. It would take so much of the guesswork out of helping others and/or ourselves, especially when it comes to meeting our own needs and those of others.

Let me once again emphasize the following purpose of emotion:

To provoke action. A certain event occurs in our life. Because of that event, we get a rush of emotion and with it comes the energy to prepare us to do whatever it is we need to do. Along with this energy comes the physiological effect it produces. We don't have to be afraid of those effects, just acknowledge the body is working the way it's supposed to, and when we experience them, know that this is a good thing.

Let us end with the focus on a more pleasant experience. Example, our first love! Do you remember?

We see someone and the cupid arrow strikes us. Our heart starts pounding. We get a big lump in our throat because of muscle tension in the neck/upper spinal areas and our mouth is dry. We are nervous and may even be shaking a little due to the uncontrolled energy flowing through our veins at this moment. You are beginning to perspire as your body temperature increases. Your heart rate and respiratory functions are also elevated. Look at the energy that is being produced in our own body at this moment. The energy you are experiencing is our heart, our mind, and our soul telling us along with every fiber of our being to meet this person. You have a strong attraction to them.

The physiological effects your body is presenting to you are giving you the very energy needed to overcome the shyness, fear, or whatever emotion may be kicking in at this point. This experience is all new to us at this age. Most being in our early

LIFESTYLE MANAGEMENT

teens, we had no reference point to these feelings/emotions. All we know is our bodies are messing us up and interfering with expressing ourselves to this new person. We may even be backing off now and shutting ourselves down by removing ourselves from the situation. Why, you might ask?

Let's imagine, or should I say, let us just recall when that happened to us. It has, to each and every single one of us. We all have experienced this, probably many times and in many situations. How can we speak the words that would describe how we feel toward this person when we are experiencing those physiological effects, not to mention that giant lump in our throat? Heck, we can barely breathe! Plus, the newness of these strange emotions that are happening to us.

How can we say the words under those circumstances, especially when our mind doesn't even have the right words because we may have not ever had those emotions before? So many things come into play with this new emotional experience which we may not understand because of the newness of this experience. What we do acknowledge is the awkwardness and fear of appearing awkward. At this age, it is a common denominator for everyone. In this stage, our bodies are changing (acne, menstrual cycles, our voices changing, all adding to the awkwardness) and we are getting new information and new internal messages.

What these emotions do, or should I say, what our brain does upon producing the emotions is to decide whether to shut us down, shy away, or act accordingly. It is this for which the energy was produced. We know consciously and subconsciously, what we need to do and want to do.

Even though this experience was new to us, in our wonderful design, we know what needs to be done. We select the appropriate actions necessary which will lead to the accomplishment of the activity(s) to gratify that which caused the emotion. This is if we have developed effectively without disruption through our prerequisite developmental stages.

What occurs when the proper action does not take place and you shy away without ever meeting this beautiful individual you are greatly attracted to? My guess is you focused more on the physiological effects and things going on with your body instead of using the energy to make the contact. We have all done this more than once, even if we have developed properly and have the necessary skills.

Next time we are in this situation, as I mentioned earlier, subconsciously, we know the energy produced first time did not lead to successful gratification of the experience. The brain, upon triggering the emotions give us even greater force and energy. Now, you have enhanced physiological symptoms to deal with. Do you remember when this happened to you and you felt like you were going to burst?

You had better do what you need to do! Put your best foot forward and make contact. We will grow more confident and secure with ourselves, with each successful experience with the appropriate use of emotions. If you decided to shut down once again, you probably already know that every time this happened, the force will get greater and greater. The energy, the power is frightening when we choose not to put ourselves in situations because the tangled, bottled up force inside overwhelms us instead of allowing us to do what emotion is designed for— *provoke action*. Appropriate action, I might add. When we choose to allow ourselves to shut down as an option, avoidance becomes a developed pattern of behavior. We all know where this leads. **To Emptiness.**

Inappropriate action does not resolve the issue, even though occasionally when the wrong action is produced, the energy is released but the problem is not solved. The result will be the same next time, except probably enhanced. When this force and energy is kept or turned inside and not released effectively, it devastates us physically, mentally, and emotionally.

I believe that unresolved emotion is what creates many of the human psyche breakdowns, as well as possibly being the root cause of many other biological illnesses. Early into my career, I became aware of something else which can happen with our emotional development. I found that our natural emotional development can and will shut down and cease to evolve during certain stages of our development if we happen to be faced with certain traumatic experiences. When things/events happen to us, which we are not yet equipped to handle, nor prepared for physically, mentally or emotionally. Such as severe prolonged illness and inappropriate treatment, abuse, mind-altering substances, developmental disorders, or traumatic brain injury. We will continue to grow physically, and if we still have the capacity, will continue to learn effectively. We will grow into attractive, intelligent adults, but emotionally, may be in what I referred to as a *stuck state*.

What I believe occurs, is when things happen to us that we have not yet developed the natural coping mechanisms to handle, we shut down emotionally. We have not had effective and appropriate growing, learning, developmental experiences to ready ourselves for certain physical and psychological experiences. So our brain does the only thing it knows to do—shutdown and block out. Whatever the emotional state that we have evolved up to at that point remains intact and ceases to evolve. The unfortunate example of this that I've seen so very often is with individuals who have been sexually abused as children. I recall one of the first cases when I came to this conclusion.

The patient was female, thirty-plus years of age, with advanced educational degree's. She was well-respected within her profession, held a managerial position in healthcare, no children, three times divorced. Over the course of her adult life, she had been in and out of psychiatric treatment facilities. The doctors were very familiar with her case. Upon completing the evaluation, I noted her activity preferences and coping mechanisms did not align chronologically. In fact, they aligned with preschool children. I shared my findings with the treatment team and her supervising doctor who had suspected sexual abuse for years.

This patient, being an intelligent, attractive, articulate, reasonable adult female, had always denied the doctors suspicions, for she had completely blocked it from her mind. Let me rephrase that, she effectively blocked it from her mind, at least for many years. She had no conscious memory or awareness of the abuse. What was also interesting in this particular case is the thing that triggered the psychiatric episode. She was driving to work one morning and she noticed a new billboard sign which was a warning about child abuse.

It was obvious her subconscious was letting her know she was at a stage in her life where she was ready. She was sharp enough and intelligent enough to do the work that was necessary for herself to get on with her life emotionally. Being in a safe, nurturing, therapeutic environment and having excellent doctors and staff available, she was able to recall and work through the trauma caused by an act that she had no control of. One of the reasons which may have led to her divorces could be the fact that she was a beautiful, intelligent, hard-working, diligent, wonderful human being who had the emotional coping mechanisms of a three to five-year-old who happened to be in a stuck state that no one was aware of until that point.

It seems to me emotional development can be remedied if our parents, our communities, and our educational systems would not compromise or interfere with our natural development, but assist with it, instead of adding to the confusion.

Fourth, the social component of self: Another unique part of our being. We are social creatures, as discussed earlier when exploring activity realms in the previous chapters. Our very existence is dependent on one another. Socially, we are each unique individuals, and although opposites do attract, we seek similarities when gathering with one another for whatever reason. We are attracted to one another. We need one another. We come together to gratify our personal needs whether it be through our work, chore, or play activity to accomplish things we need to in life. We all have social preferences. We don't have to be labeled a racist just because we have certain preferences. The key is acknowledging the differences and recognizing them just for that. Also, knowing that we are all God's creatures.

LIFESTYLE MANAGEMENT

All species tend to have territorial (social) boundaries. As humans, because of our social preferences, the boundaries fluctuate depending on the circumstance. For example, if you are attending a concert and you are in a crowded auditorium, it's okay to be rubbing elbows and bumping against others. Another example is walking down an empty street and one person approaches from a distance. The closer you get the more anxiety builds up until you cross your paths. Or imagine this, you are in a crowded elevator. It is okay to be scrunched up against somebody else. Everybody gets off the next floor, except for you and the person standing right beside you. They do not move. Moments ago, that was fine. Now, the anxiety level is great. Our territorial boundaries fluctuate that quickly and readily depending on circumstances that we are in.

This is another area similar to the emotional component of self, although an external factor adds a different element. Here, too, we can also cease to develop socially by not developing appropriate social skills and coping mechanisms at the proper time during the developmental stages, due to certain situations or circumstances we happen to be exposed to.

There are lessons I learned very early in life from my mother which have echoed so loudly in my own psyche for as long as I can remember. I took them to heart, probably to a fault, according to my older brothers and sisters. Those words, those wonderful teachings that I held in my mind and heart all my life. One was "You have to learn to stand on your own two feet." (In reference to facing up to others and your responsibilities.) Two was "You have to fight your own battles." Three was "Always be considerate and respectful of others." (This reminds me of one of my favorite verses in scripture, Philippians 4:4.)

Number two was the one that got me in trouble way too often.

What important lessons these are! The first, I am sure, represented many things. What she was telling us was to *trust and rely on ourselves. Know what and who you are and have confidence in yourself when dealing with others.* Know that you are going to be all right, no matter what others say or do.

I think the greater lesson is respect of oneself and what you believe in and do what is necessary to get along in life. How many parents today are teaching their children to be righteous and to stand firm? To be righteous toward one and all, instead of so much of the self-righteousness we see today. How many are teaching them lessons we don't get in our schools, society, government, and social media?

We are getting so many messages from everywhere, with advanced technology we are instantly and continuously barraged by information. Much may lack righteousness, modesty, decency, commitment, restraint, and higher moral standards.

Socially, we are all unique and different in so many ways. They say opposites attract and I agree with this. I believe when we were created, some of us were designed in such a manner as to be incomplete. What I mean by this is we are lacking in some areas; an incompleteness of our very makeup. Purposely, I might add. So when we find our true soul mate and connect, we grow together, fill each other's voids, and due to the sacrament of matrimony do become one who is more complete.

On the other hand, socially, we always tend to be attracted to and seek similarities.

Well, here I go, I will be getting on my soapbox now and diverting away from the subject matter—the components of self. As I stated in the last few paragraphs, as our society moves away from righteousness, restraint, modesty, and morality, we are truly getting further and further away from that healthy and productive society which our founding fathers conceived when developing our constitutional guidelines for this nation.

We are getting too far away from the people we were designed and intended to be, forsaking our very design and pursuing not what comes from within, but that which is external. We seek what the world and our society tell us we should be seeking. What we want, is what the world and society show us and tell us we should want. All this does and is expected to do is draw our energy, our thoughts, and actions away from our purpose and destiny, drawing us further and further away from the person we have been created to be.

This leads us to our next marvelous being.

Fifth, the spiritual component of self: This component, as all the others, is another unique and separate entity within us. For those of us of faith, especially those of Christian faith recognizing the trinity—the Father, Son, and Holy Spirit—the spirit is the gift, part of the living God in each and every one of us. This component of self can supersede all the others when necessary. All we have to do is acknowledge it and accept it!

I wish I had the right words—the inspiring words—that would cause a more complete knowledge and understanding of this component. I can only describe it abstractly. We feel it, we sense it, we are moved to great emotion by it, people are healed by it. The things that happen within and around us, we can only describe as miracles, because science has no answer or explanation. The real key is deciding within ourselves whether this is fate or faith. If we are going to wait until we know, it will be too late.

Many years ago, when my children were in middle school and high school, one evening at the dinner table, I asked a question for all to consider and then share their thoughts. The question was: *Which is better, knowledge or belief?*

It brought up some interesting comments and brief discussion. Basically, it was four against one—my spouse and three children chose knowledge. For the defense of knowledge was, *if you know it, its fact; you have proof, it has been proven.*

The next question I asked my loved ones was this: *What do you know that you would die for?*

Silence!

After a few moments, I asked another question which was this: *Would you die for what you believe in?*

Let's just say, I was pleased with their answers and responses. I will end this component of self with this comment which is another quote from the scripture Matthew 6:33, "Seek first the kingdom of God and his righteousness and all else will be rendered unto you."

This lets us know we are not forgotten and the Spirit is always with us. Let us accept that and rejoice. This is a sacred gift! Personally, I like to think of it as a homing device. This is one device I won't suggest shutting off.

Five Components of Self: (quick review)

1. *Physical component*
2. *Intellectual component*
3. *Emotional component*
4. *Social component*
5. *Spiritual component*

Nurture each and every component of yourself; you are worth it. Each is a key to developing a productive lifestyle management plan. Ending this chapter on components of self, I would like to quote a comment made by Pope Francis in a tweet on May 9, 2017, "Everyone has something to give society; no one is excluded from contributing to the good of all."

Since we're talking about our society and social aspects, let us move on. Let this lead us into another major limiting factor. This will be a good time to move on to the next chapter.

Chapter 10

Socialization

There is no argument and no debate on whether or not we are all social creatures. Very few, if any, ever truly live independent of everyone else. I am willing to go as far to say no one has ever lived totally independent of other people.

Imagine, if you will, the frontiersman of old. Before they set out, they gathered together all the supplies they needed, which they got from someone else. Off to the wild, blue yonder, heading west into the sunset!

They may have set off alone and their hermitage may have lasted several days, weeks, occasionally maybe even for several months. Eventually, supplies like gunpowder, ammunition, flour, and other necessities would dwindle. They would need to come in contact with others to trade for the supplies they needed to allow themselves to continue their lifestyle as independently as they preferred.

Let's say you were in solitary confinement. Hopefully, you will never be in this situation. You are isolated in your own cell by yourself. You will still have contact directly and indirectly for meals, sanitation, and other personal requirements as needed. As you can see by these two examples, no one is truly completely independent of others. We are all interconnected and interdependent on one another.

Earlier when we were defining activity categories we found through involvement in social interactive types of activity, all of our needs are met—learning, procreation, food, transportation, recreation, and on and on.

We can go on forever exploring how we are interconnected and reliant on one another in so many ways. It would take more than a few chapters and more than likely be an unending process. It would be interesting, but lead us nowhere.

What has always fascinated, intrigued, and perplexed me is our interdependence. We live in crowded cities, in fairly tight, compact communities. We trade with every country on earth. Despite our close proximity to one another and our willingness to benefit from one another via trade, services, etc., we are constantly at war with one another. We are killing one another in so many ways literally and figuratively for any number of reasons. I throw up my hands in wonder! Maybe I will just start reaching out my hand in greeting.

Let's begin this exploration of our complex social self and our social needs.

I have done much research back in my college days and throughout my career. The literature identified and in classes as well as lectures, we discussed the four basic social needs. I have added a fifth! Shortly after I began my professional career at a community mental health center, I found there was one other thing that drew people together. This thing was not described or interrelated with the other four.

Before we go any further, let us take a look at what I refer to as the, *Five Basic Social Needs*.

We all have them, we all have built into our makeup a desire to gratify them. Whether we do or not, is a different story. Here we will review the five and determine whether or not we effectively gratify our own social needs. The basic five are a guide and an excellent starting point to see if we have a productive social support system.

These are the *five basic social needs*:

1. *Intimacy:* I will describe this as a higher level of human encounter. A relationship that usually arouses the elements of empathy, love, and true caring within us. Let us not confuse intimacy with sexual arousal, though it is nice when they can go together. But I

LIFESTYLE MANAGEMENT

guess you can go to the red light district, pay whatever the going rate may be, and have all the sexual contact you wish. I guarantee you will not get a penny's worth of intimacy.

We can be intimate with anyone—spouses, best friends, family members, clergy, colleagues, mentor, or whomever. You know when you are in or have an intimate relationship. It is when you can share anything—your deepest, darkest secrets and concerns—openly and not worry about being looked down upon, frowned upon, put down, or rejected. Your intimate relationships can always be relied on. These relationships are wonderful and extremely beneficial. The fact is, the average person may only have, at best, ten people in their entire lifetime they can truly say they have been intimate with. If we ever have one, two, or three intimate friends or people at any given time in our life, folks, we could share anything and everything. We really have got it made.

Imagine being able to say anything no matter how difficult: your deepest feelings, thoughts, ideas, etc. Imagine if you could talk about your darkest, most hidden secrets and concerns and be able to share them openly with somebody. It reminds me of a movie that came out many years ago. You may recollect the first *Crocodile Dundee* movie. There is a scene when the writer/reporter is first meeting with Mr. Dundee in an outback bar. She's questioning him about the fact that they have no resources, no cities, and no clinics around. She asked a question about what to do when he needs to get help, insinuating counseling and psychological assistance. When our star character finally understands what she's asking and getting at, he says the classic line! The line which I loved then and now. It just makes sense. I smile when I hear it or think about even now. It relates so very well to what we are talking about here. He says in his outback Australian accent, "Oh, I getcha! When you got somethin' to hide, you tell Wally!" The reporter looks at him, then at a gentleman telling stories to a group of people gathered around him at the bar. Of course, Wally is the local gossip, embellishing all his stories. She looks bewildered as she remarks, "You tell him?" Of course, she is wondering why. Then she asks, "Why?" Crocodile Dundee says matter-of-factly, "Well, if you're in trouble or somethin's troublin' ya, ya just tell Wally. When you tell him, next thing you know, everyone in the entire outback, knows your secrets and what you're hidin', so then you have nothing to hide anymore."

The point I would like to make with this example is that when people know the difficulty we are having, they can decide the best way to help, or whether or not they want to help. In either case, you know what your next course of action should be.

Having people in our lives where we can share things comfortably saves everyone a lot of trouble. We need to develop intimate relationships throughout our life. They may change, they may come and go, but they will always be a cherished and valuable commodity when we have them at our disposal, and we at theirs.

2. *Recreative.* People seek others who have similar recreational interest. This is the most common reason we interact with other people and why we select our friends. These are people who we share similar interests with so when we have time to spend together, we can pursue those interests. This is where we spend the majority of our unobligated time. This happens to be the only expenditure in our budgets that when added up together will make the nation's defense and healthcare budget look small. I know, you are saying, this guy is off his rocker right about now. Aren't you?

Let's think about this for moment. Take a look at your last paystub. How much did the federal government take out? I will use twenty percent for our figure. Let's say, that ends up being a couple of hundred dollars. Yeah, I know some of you are laughing pretty hard now. You know what my take home pay is.

Of that twenty percent, think of all the things that is going to cover in reference to the expenses of our federal government. It's bills, services, paying the employees, and of course, we can go on and on. Let us just jump to the defense of our nation and stop there for all intents and purposes. How much of that twenty percent is actually going to the defense budget? I'm not an economist nor an accountant or bean counter. If you take all $200 for the defense budget, that won't come close to what the average person spends on their own recreation. Example, I spend almost that much on our cable and Internet bill, and I don't even like watching TV or getting on the computer. I'm willing to bet many people spend that much just going out to eat. I know one ski trip for an average family would be ten times that. One evening at the movies with your date is probably going to cost you more than fifty dollars. See what I mean? We are not even talking about the cost of the membership at the Health club, tennis club, country club, book of the month club, or wine tasters' club. Shall I go on? I think not. You're getting the point!

We place a lot of value on our leisure activities in pursuit of recreation which we all need at consistent and regular intervals to keep ourselves healthy, refreshed, and productive. Recreation is second to intimacy as far as social value. In fact, it is through our recreational pursuits, when we're having fun and enjoying our experience with one another, can lead to the start of our intimate relationships. We learn we can let our hair down and truly be ourselves and see each other in the same situation and same manner as well. It is the environment where we can test, challenge, and compete with one another and see each other's true colors. It's a great testing ground for selecting and considering whether to develop intimate relationships.

3. *Work:* Many of you may be asking why work is a basic social need, especially after following the first two. In reference to what I mentioned earlier, we all have our jobs and our work to do no matter what age we happen to be. Work is what draws many people together every day. Work consumes a majority of our day throughout a typical week. We all have a desire to be productive in some way. It is in our makeup and design to develop and use the gifts and talents we have been given; to use them to make

SOCIALIZATION

our way and earn our keep, and as I stated many times already, to find our purpose.

Granted, this is not always the most productive area to be social, especially compared to the first two social needs. Work is more of a societal need and expectation. For most of us, it is the largest social unit that we have. Many of us may come in contact with more people at work each day than we do in any other area of our life. Many of us may develop wonderful and long-lasting relationships through our work environment, although this is not why we are there. We are there to produce whatever it is the job requires we produce. We are not there to socialize for our own intent and purpose. In fact, we may be facing lawsuits, reprimands, or even being fired by pursuing our own social interests in this environment. What we do get from work is a strong sense of self and dignity by having a means to provide for ourselves and families and not being a burden to society.

4. *Service:* This is the one that I mentioned you will probably not find in any literature until now. I will explain the reason I added this domain to the basic social needs. It became very apparent to me early in my professional life. Although thinking about it now, the wheels probably started turning and the seeds planted in my college days when I started volunteering my time and services for various causes. I found that there are people out there willing to utilize their time and talents at no expense to the cause or individuals in need. The organizations in which I worked, I decided to utilize volunteers for a variety of reasons and tasks to assist at my job. I was working for a MR/MH organization, serving people with a wide variety of physical and cognitive impairments. Within the workplace we could find ourselves in some interesting situations. In ah (How can I say this delicately?) let's just say, some sensitive environments. Which were not always the safest or most respectable places to be, if you get my drift. Many times it can be very stressful. I was always very careful about the interview process when searching for volunteers to work in such unique, sensi-

tive environments. One of the questions I would always ask is "Why are you interested in doing this?" The responses I heard so often were: "Well, I get more out of it than what I put in," "It is gratifying to be able to help others," "I just like helping other people."

After hearing these statements so often during the selecting process and evaluation of volunteers and relating to them myself, I began to wonder. Knowing some of our volunteers not only put a lot of time into direct service assistance, they also spent a lot of time in preparation, and some spent a lot of their own funds to provide a service without any expectation of reimbursement. I really began to question the statement, "I get more out of it than what I put in."

Where did this fit in with the four basic social needs? I began to question myself further. This is not their work. They are not here to socialize for recreational or their spiritual development nor for personal intimacy. If they were, that would be very misguided and we would figure that out quickly. We'd move them to another environment or dismiss them. They are not paid, "although it is very much like work". So why? What draws people to want to give so much of their own time, energy, money, and yes, in many cases, even the draining of their emotions to assist others? It didn't fit in the categories of the four basic social needs.

I decided there must be another driving force within us. I started to refer to it as the *service connection*. I believe we all have an innate desire to be of benefit to others. To be able to assist and help others and to be of service to one another without attaching a price tag.

Over the course of my career, I asked this question to thousands of people in treatments settings; patients, staff, family members; at lectures, presentations, workshops, and conferences throughout the country. I have asked individuals and literally anyone I could when the opportunity arose, mainly just to confirm my theory of the basic social needs. I would like to say the response was always unanimous to the question that I'm about to state, and I want you to ask yourself the same question. Then pause for a few moments to reflect on your answer.

The question is this: "If you knew you could do something for someone and knew it would benefit them, even though it might set you back a little because of cost or some time, would you help?" The answer would *almost* always be yes. The answers in response to the question looked like these: "Of course" or "I always had." I can't say a hundred percent. Keep in mind, I had asked thousands of people this question. I have a running tab of those individuals who, for whatever reason, put a contingency on that statement. Only five to this point put a contingency on that statement. Those contingencies, when explored with these five individuals, were placed on *one* particular person only. It was either a family member, in-law, or in one case, a next-door neighbor. Other than that particular individual in those five people's lives, even they identified absolutely that they would want to help and have done so. If anyone needs more convincing or justification for why I have added this to our 4 Basic Social Needs you may want to refer to Galatians 5, 13–14.)

Exploring the reasons why those particular individuals excluded family or certain individuals actually reinforces my original statement when outlining the term "work." I'll explain. When, we are constantly doing things for family this is part of our duties and responsibilities making it fall under the work/job definition. As all of us know, doing our job for family, friends, or even a neighbor can be and is a constantly demanding and at times thankless task. In these cases, we are doing it without any expectation of anything from our efforts other than being dutiful to our family and a good neighbor. Excessive amounts of time spent in non-gratified activity, whatever the situation we may be performing them in, will eventually lead to feelings of anger, bitterness, and resentfulness.

We are a service-driven society. We love to do things that will benefit other people. The fact remains that when service is provided and continued for an extended period of time, and we see that the benefactor is not benefiting or improving from it, the desire to continue is diminished. Once we see and acknowledge that it is not benefiting them, resentment occurs. What comes to mind is the phrase, "throwing it down a rat hole."

This makes us all very frustrated and/or angry at those individuals, for we get the sense that they do not want to help themselves. We get the sense that they don't appreciate our efforts. We get the sense that we are being used. Whereas, on the other hand, if we see it does help, they are learning, they are improving, they are moving on, and becoming less dependent. That is a very gratifying experience worthy of all of our efforts. Thus, enhancing the desire to be of benefit to one another versus being taken advantage of.

In one situation, the service connection benefits and enhances both parties. The other drains one and makes the other more dependent and less self-reliant, making them less able to manage their own life productively.

5. *Spirituality:* This is another major reason people get together, literally by the billions each week. We all seek our creator in some way, shape, and form. We all have a need and desire to gather with other like-minded people to explore our spirituality. We gather to share in our beliefs. Even atheists will seek and find others who have no belief to acknowledge and confirm their belief system. They may even go to great lengths to get others away from actively gratifying their spiritual needs so as not to feel isolated and alone in their belief system. This is unfortunate when this occurs, for neither is satisfied, destinies and purposes are not fulfilled, and one's fate may be sealed.

You have just been presented with five basic social needs. That doesn't mean there are not others; there may be. These are just the basics. Maybe in the future, I or someone else will identify others. We are very complex social creatures as we explained earlier in this book. No other species known to man is as socially diverse. We gather to live in large communes (communities, neighborhoods, cities) to raise and protect our families. We spend the majority of our day in large social contact situations,

SOCIALIZATION

our work environments, social clubs, and organizations. We gather to share in our diverse interests (sports, cultural events, concerts, fairs, and festivals). We learn in large social environments (schools and universities). We gather together for worship, living, loving, learning, working, caring for others, and yet, yes, so unfortunately, warring.

When we have strong and productive support systems, meaning not only are our own social needs being met, but we in turn are meeting the needs of others in our lives, we thrive. When we are not meeting our basic social needs, we do not thrive. In fact, we may become ill when deprived of any of the basic five. If not physically ill, it can affect us in any number of ways which may not be readily apparent to ourselves or others except within our individual internal being. In such case, it may affect our own self perceptions of which we have no understanding. Isn't that interesting?

The unique individuals that we are, need others to gain our own self perceptions, by how others respond, interact, or lack thereof toward us.

What I would like for each one of you to do now is get a piece of paper and outline your own present social support system. List all the social connections you have for whatever reason. Start with the largest and go to the smallest. Let me give you an example. See list below.

* Work
* Church
* Family
* Professional organization membership
* Neighbors
* Health club membership
* Friends

When your list is complete, it may look something similar to this. These are very typical for an average adult during their productive years. Make sure you haven't left anything or, anyone out.

LIFESTYLE MANAGEMENT

Now number one through five, representing which basic social need is being met or gratified by this particular social unit. See example below.

Example:

	Basic Social Needs
#3 Work	
#5 Church	1- Intimacy
#3, #1 Family	2- Recreative
#3 Professional organization membership	3- Work
#4 Neighbors	4- Service
#2 Health club membership	5- Spiritual
#2, #1 Friends	

Next step, place a plus (+) sign before the ones that you feel are satisfactorily meeting your needs. Place a minus (-) sign before the ones not satisfactorily meeting your needs. If the connection exists, although there is no expectation for meeting or not meeting any of your social needs, it is just there, leave it blank. (Example see below, Family or if you included your 1500 social media contacts or the checkout clerk at a store you frequent. If they are not meeting any of your basic social needs, leave them blank,)

Example:

+ Work
- Church
  Family
- Professional Org. / Memberships
- Neighbors
- Health Club membership
  Friends

SOCIALIZATION

You may have found that some of your social needs are not actually being met as effectively as you thought or not as much as you would have suspected from that certain social unit(s). They might have initially served you very well. Once you explore each item further, you may find they or you have changed, died, moved away or just moved on or chose to go down a different path. Whether it be circumstances, interest, likes, dislikes, things and people (it/they) grow, learn, or evolve into different stages. All of which bring about changes in each of us and our relationships with one another.

As you can see in this second example, maybe our spiritual needs are not being met the way we would like for them to. The family connection may not be meeting our social expectations. It sure is nice when our spouses are truly our kindred spirit and we can be intimate, sharing and confiding our deepest and darkest thoughts, secrets, and desires, and not being worried about being frowned upon or developing grounds for divorce. This is not always the case, unfortunately. Look at the current divorce rate. Let me divert for a moment to say this. Due to human complexity and differences in interest, style and preferences, no one person can meet all of our social needs, not even the basics of another person, no matter how much you love and care for them. This is an unrealistic expectation. Healthy relationships allow for each other's growth and privacy. That is what the BFF's are for.

Getting back to examples:

We are in our professional organization(s) because we want to continue to develop our skills and update our knowledge base, or our job requires it of us. Other than working on projects and meeting our continuing education requirements, it's probably not that socially productive for us, either.

Yes, we are very lucky if we have wonderful neighbors. Other than just waving to them or having brief casual conversations with them while getting your mail, you may not have much contact with them unless they need your help to carry something from their second floor down to the basement or vice versa, and we need them for a similar task.

With the health club connection, I may pay my dues even though it is unlikely that you, I should say I am not there more than once or twice a week at best to get a quick workout. It's mainly to relieve stress and hopefully keep at a fairly conditioned level. I say "Hello" when arriving; "See you next time," upon leaving. Depending on the age of an individual and where they are in their life, we may not have as much contact with our friends as we once did. This is mainly due to a lack of contact as we get older.

So how productive is your support system? Is it gratifying the basic five effectively? If it is not, not to worry, it is an easy fix.

It will take time, energy, commitment, and possibly even a tap into your resources. I can assure you it is always well worth the investment in the long run. Using the five basic social needs as our starting point and base to build on, makes it an easy process to develop or redevelop our support systems. It's a good guide to help assure that you are considering each of the basic social needs effectively.

When people have been in their ritualistic routines and set in their ways and habits for long periods of time, it can be difficult to make changes. When their lifestyle has become ingrained, taking the initial steps can be difficult.

My entire career working with populations that were experiencing severe difficulties and had more than likely already isolated themselves. This makes the process of taking those initial steps a real struggle, they will need lots of encouragement and coaching. As part of the treatment process, it may take a little more guidance and a set of built-in experimental situations before they can take the initial steps and commit to the path of developing a social support system that works for them. For a healthy population, once you commit and take the first steps, the fun begins.

Many have asked me, "Well, where do I begin?" "How and where do I start to connect?" "Outside of work and/or family, I've had no social life."

As mentioned in the previous paragraphs, reviewing the basics and determining what is lacking is always a good place to start. By developing the social unit(s) that may have been missing or were not being gratified, not only will you start to gratify your basic social needs, you are also developing a broader support system. With that,

SOCIALIZATION

you are also more than likely creating a more productive balance in your life.

If you already have determined which one you would like to start with first, that is fine. For those who have been out of touch, outside of family and work environment or have been an inpatient in the hospital environment, I usually suggest starting with the most nonthreatening of the basic social needs. I am going to pause here for a moment and have you review the five basic social needs. Then, I am going to take you through a ranking system in reference to social value and difficulty factor to obtain and gratify effectively each of the basic five.

#1 Intimacy: It is the most difficult to obtain and is the most valuable of social experiences. The most bang for the buck!, this is the gold standard!

#2 Recreation: For adults, it is the second most difficult to obtain. It is also second when it comes to being the most valuable for the very reasons mentioned earlier. This area helps maintain health and balance, and keeps us refreshed, not to mention being enjoyable. And when we have fun doing whatever it is we're doing with others, we are more likely to do it again, always making this a good place to begin.

Note: This is usually very easy for young people and those who have recently reached the specialization stage up to thirty years of age. Once we begin the process of raising our families, for the next several years of our life or until we have completed the raising of our children, this becomes more difficult for a couple of reasons:

One: The time commitment shifts and changes as we care for the needs of our young ones.

Two: Finding people who have the same interests may be difficult. This task can be made easier by going to places that interest us, or joining certain clubs or organizations. This instantly puts you in contact with folks who have similar interests. Example, you like to ski but don't know anyone who skis.

LIFESTYLE MANAGEMENT

Joining the ski club automatically brings you in contact with others who have the same interest you do.

Three: Not only do we have to find folks who have a similar interests, once we find them, it is best if we find folks who have a similar skill level in that activity. That way, both are sure to have a good experience. As with most activities, it's most pleasant and enjoyable when participating with somebody who has the same skill level, or at least close to. Have you ever played table tennis with someone who's a whole lot better than you? It's no fun. What about racquetball? You may stand there watching the ball as it whizzes by when you are playing someone a whole lot better than you. It's no fun.

The same also works in reverse. Did you ever play chess with someone who is not even close to your skill level? It's no fun. What about golf? Did you ever play someone who is not even close to your skill? I haven't. My golf game is terrible.

The game of golf is wonderful and progressive. It even has a handicapping system to level the playing field, as well as the scorecards so as not to embarrass those of us who are not great players and to help us equalize our game with those we happen to be playing with. I have played golf with people who are better than me, that includes almost everyone. They are not having much fun waiting for me. I usually tell them to play on, I'll meet them at the clubhouse. By the time I get there, they are long gone. The bartender had to call a taxi for them because they could legally be responsible if they were to be allowed to drive home.

#3 Work: Work is right in the middle. It does have a high societal value, although not so much for personal social gratification. It does enhance one's sense of self and self-esteem. As far as its difficulty factor ranking, it is also in the middle. We have to have something to offer. A skill set that someone is willing to pay us for.

#4 Service: This is a very easy one to get involved with. All we need is a willingness and some time to give. This can also be a very gratifying experience without being threatening. You are there

SOCIALIZATION

to provide a specific service, and all you need to do is give your time or do the task expected. You set the parameters of how much time, so it becomes a win-win for our time investment. Finding a place to volunteer is not difficult. Believe me, there are a 1,000 organizations out in our many communities that would be more than happy to have an hour of your time. It does not matter what your skills may be.

As an example, if you would be willing to spend time with a person, let's say, in a nursing home, it may be someone who generally has no visitors. They may not even be able to communicate with you. Just being there, talking to them, holding their hand, reading to them, or even just being still and spending time with them can make a big difference to that person and you. This service social need does not place us in those awkward situations which many social activities can. Some examples of this is where one party may expect some sort of commitment from the other whereas the feeling is not mutual. Or one individual wants to do things the other party is not wishing to.

#5 Spiritually: This one is ranked last only due to the difficulty factor. It is the easiest to get involved with. All you have to do is go! Go to a church or place of worship when there is a service and attend. No expectations, just an opportunity to be with a large number of people who are sharing one thing in common. That common denominator is seeking to better understand the Creator.

The unique thing about this example is, every church I have attended has lots of extracurricular activities. Some are very elaborate and have their own recreational facilities. There are generally youth through adult education programs. Some even have staff to coordinate activities to meet the needs and interests of members of various age groups in the congregation. There more than likely will be numerous volunteer opportunities within the parish itself, and many have outreach programs that extend into the community. Even the little church that my family and I attend when we are vacationing in the mountains has a variety of different activities to partake in. This little parish has entertainment, picnics, choirs, singing and community projects. It's so small that when my family is in attendance, we are about half of the congregation. There are only five of us and Grandma!

Once we commit to develop our social support system, even if we start with the simplest one to get involved in, it may lead to many, if not all the other basic social need components being met. If we decide we want to get involved a little more extensively just by exposing ourselves to other people, we may find folks who have the same or very similar interests that we have. This, in turn, may lead us to other things, such as job opportunities, recreational opportunities, friendships, and yes, even the hierarchy. *Intimate relationships.*

As we come in contact with others and begin to communicate, share, and confide with other like-minded in our spiritual beliefs, one step forward with the least threatening of the five basic social units can blossom into a very productive, balanced social support system.

I now want to reemphasize this one concept. Understand that every individual is unique and also the fact that there are very many people who are fiercely independent. You may have already known that about yourself or maybe have just discovered this upon taking the group benefit exercise. What I know about those individuals who score high in *freedom,* they are usually very independent. If they choose to isolate themselves or just refuse to ask for assistance or help because it goes against their grain, they can end up being very frustrated. Being one of those individuals, I finally came to the realization that the more connected I am with others for various reasons to meet their needs, or they to meet mine, the more independent I become. When isolated and dependent solely on myself, I find myself less independent and less able to accomplish things that I need to accomplish and, in many cases, unable to do the very things I need to do and want to do.

So keep this in mind. For all those who may feel or want to be self-sufficient, the more connections you have for whatever reason, give or take, the more able you are going to be to accomplish whatever it is you need to accomplish. You may find, just like I have, some of your best relationships have evolved out of your own needs. Remember these gems? "Ask and you shall receive; Seek and you will find; Knock and the door will be opened." "When two or more gather in my name, I will be in thy midst."

What is this telling us? These scripture verses are telling us, to get together, be connected, and share with one another, especially in reference to our Lord and earnest needs.

Chapter 11

Desocialization

We spent the last chapter of this book talking about the importance of social interaction, basic social needs, and effective ways to develop our social support systems. In this chapter, we will explore what I refer to as the *desocialization process*. This is the way our society has been structured and set up for probably the last hundred years or so. It could and does lead us down a path of desocialization.

I am about to guide you through the social developmental stages which align with our age and social structure. It is not only interesting, it is imperative to understand, knowing where we are within this socialization/desocialization scale (as I like to refer to it), that I'm about to present to you. I will explain more about that once we go through all the stages. Let's begin this socialization journey that our societal structure sets us all up for.

If there was ever a time during our existence where we all are truly created equal, it is at birth. Now, keep in mind throughout this chapter, I am speaking specifically and only in social terms. We are not created equal, except in God's eyes only. Some are rich, some are poor, some short, some tall, some are very intelligent, some not so intelligent. Some are born with ten fingers and ten toes, some are not; some are born with that silver spoon in their mouth, some are not; some have great paying jobs, some do not; some are great artists, some are not; and some have great athletic ability, some do not. As you can see, we are not equal by any means. As I began with this paragraph, the only time we are actually equal across the board with everyone else is at birth. Again, I reference equal only in the social radiance of the infant child. There is an uninhibitedness socially with the infant. It is such a radiance that it affects all who are around it. With the world being an open book socially, there are no preconceived expectations or prejudice.

Here, we will begin to run through the desocialization process. Ten stages we all go through in reference to our openness and comfort socially.

Infancy stage (day of birth to one and a half years of age) In this stage, socially, we have no inhibitors. We can do anything anywhere, and we will be accepted by all. Were you ever in a room with a number of people? Let's say, adults. Someone walks in with a baby! Instantly, you see a change. People who were very formal a moment ago are now making strange sounds and noises when speaking with the child, laughing, carrying on.

The innocence, openness, and uninhibitedness the infant brings, is what I term *social radiance*. When it is present, as it is with all in this stage, it breaks down all social barriers we had in place. We can all let our hair down and act any way we choose. Whereas, if we were to be in the same environmental situations without the infant, it would be very awkward and uncomfortable if someone would begin to talk funny or make weird sounds or gestures. This stage may last at least for several months, and in rare cases, longer if that child is in a very nurturing environment. In this stage, we are a well-rounded social being. All of our needs are being met. All are equal!

Toddler stage (six months to two-plus years) During this stage, as soon as the infant begins to understand language, gestures, and/ or people, the infant starts to associate certain things with certain people. Example, food, comfort, and security with Mom, play and bedtime stories with Dad. Parents try to instill in their children things that are acceptable and not acceptable. We may start potty training them. What was fine just a few weeks or months ago—defecating, urinating in their diaper or anywhere they please at any time –isn't any more, now it is a, no no.

LIFESTYLE MANAGEMENT

In the last stage when the infant finished its bottle or its meal, it got a nice pat on the back, let out a big ole belch, and was praised for doing so. Now, in the latter part of this stage, it is not a good idea, especially at the table or in public places.

We start learning to walk. This can be a frightening time for a child. They start learning about fear and trust.

Do you remember the look in your own children's eyes when you helped them stand upright? The other parent was just a few feet away with arms extended, while the other supported the infant under the arms, then said, "Walk to Mommy." Remember the look in the child's eye, especially when Dad let go? Remember how big those eyes were, and how you could see the apprehension and fear? Standing on one's own two feet at this stage can be a frightening experience. It's a long way to the floor. They instinctively know something bad might happen. Do you recall the first chapter discussion about our instincts and how they are designed to protect us?

By hearing "No" so often, the toddler begins to understand the world is not an open book anymore. All people are not safe to be around. The desocialization process has begun, and we are only a few months to a few years old.

Preschool stage (three to five years) Now that we are a few years old and have some social experience under our belt, we may even get punished or disciplined when we let out a big ole belch or wet our pants or bed. What was okay not too long ago in our young life is now a punishable offense—jail time, time out, stay in your room. When they start to speak, we instruct our children what to say, how, when, and where to say such things as "Thank you", "Please", "Yes", "No", etc. Some of the words we may have said earlier, and not quite understanding what they meant, may have gotten laughs and giggles. Now, we get spanked for saying the same words. Jail time!

We start teaching the child what is proper and what is not, socially speaking. We tell them to stay close to us when out and never talk to strangers. Never get into an automobile with a stranger. We start to realize that there is a time and place for everything depending on the social situations. That there are people we should not always

DESOCIALIZATION

trust. The desocialization process continues. The social life is still blending well with signs of some separations.

Elementary school stage (five to thirteen years of age) During this stage, a large chunk is taken out of our social radiance. Now, for the largest part of our waken day, we are in a large social environment with other children our own age. During this time, we are taught that it's not okay to interact freely. Think about this, we have been placed in a large social environment—a classroom—in close proximity of our friends and children our own age. The most natural thing to do is to interact and play with each other. We are curious of what the others are doing, that is a given. When we do so during class time we are punished. We are being taught that it is only okay to interact at certain times and in certain places.

Do you remember some of the punishments that you may have endured or experienced when you were in school for talking to the person next to you? I guess I'm talking about the old days. If you're not over fifty years of age, some of these things you may not relate to. Who knows what they are doing in these modern-day classrooms with all the social media going on? Unfortunately, probably not a whole lot of purposeful interaction.

I remember one teacher who, if you were talking to the person next to you or interacting in some appropriate or inappropriate way, she would send you to the coat room. We had to stay until she said it was okay to come out. I used to enjoy sitting on the windowsill, looking outside when I did my time in there. Sometime throughout the year, the teacher stopped doing that for no apparent reason. I knew for a while there, a lot of children were missing things from their lunch boxes. Why didn't I think of that?

Another teacher would have us stand in a corner of the room. Some teachers had us stand outside the classroom in the hall for all to see. Other teachers made us stay in at recess writing on the bulletin board, "I will not speak in class" or "I will not disrupt class" or similar assignments. Others made us stay after school to wash the chalkboards or clean erasers and we'd miss the bus and have to walk home. Those that lived in the city didn't have it so bad, for me that was a 3 mile walk home. The worst experience for me that I can recall, was when the teacher would make us stand beside her desk in front of the classroom, facing our classmates. This was a social embarrassment, to be put on display in such a manner. Not to mention the consequences that would inevitably follow. Shortly! I would fully intend, with every bit of strength and determination in my stubborn little being, to stay there solemnly until I was told to sit down or when the class would be dismissed. I knew what was going to happen. As soon as I would look up at my classmates smiling, pointing, trying to make me laugh, I would eventually give in. I could not help but laugh. As soon as I did, the whole class would burst out in loud laughter. As the teacher was dragging me by the arm to the principal's office, leaving the classroom door wide open so the whole school could hear the disruption from the class, she would state to the principal, "This young man was disrupting class," and of course the disruption could still be heard all the way to the principal's office. The consequences were never good. Jail time!

Of course, we all understand why we are put in this large social unit for the majority of our waken day and taught it's not okay to interact. Right? Because there are a certain number of things that we have to learn in this system and society during the hours we spend in school.

I grew up in an environment with nine other children and two parents. My first five years of life, I learned, if you had an issue, you dealt with it here and now. If you didn't resolve your conflict immediately and had an attitude any length of time, you not only had one person on your case, you had eleven. Being the youngest, I could ill afford nor effectively protect myself of any ill consequences of any unresolved issues. If you get my drift.

In school, that philosophy, that approach, let's just say, definitely did not work to my advantage. Oh yes, we learn a lot in our school systems. Hopefully, one of those lessons is self-control. Socially, we may take a hit. I shall repeat myself here. For the first time in our life, for the majority of our waken day, we're forced into a large social environment. We choose to sit next to people we know or want to know. The teachers catch on to that pretty quickly. That is usually when they bring out the alphabetical order of seating system and

DESOCIALIZATION

separate you. That is all fine and good, but here we are in a large social environment with kids our own age. We are around people we know or want to know, and taught it's not okay to interact. Most of us recover quite nicely, some may not. Lord knows I didn't! I will not share the damage I suffered! Ah ah ah.

I am compelled to tell this story. It is true of my sixth grade experience. The sixth-grade teacher at the school I attended was a noted disciplinarian, to put it mildly. She passed away sometime during the summer before my entering sixth-grade year. I won't say what I thought. Let me just say this, I wasn't dreading going back to school that year quite as much. Apparently, it was too late to find a teacher to fill this position. The woman they asked to fill in and teach the class (we will call her Ms. Bailey) was in her seventies, she had long since retired. Ms. Bailey had done her homework!

When we came to the school that fall, and upon reporting to our classroom, we were greeted by the new teacher. The classroom was set up traditionally—row after row of desks. As always, we selected seats next to our friends or people we wanted to be friends with. Fully expecting by the end of the school week, we would be in alphabetical order once again. What occurred was something totally different. This teacher who we knew nothing of, apparently knew us pretty well. What she did was not short of remarkable. She selected groups for us to be in; each group had a student who was good in math, a student who was good in English and a student who was good in science. Each had a student who was a good artist; I'll claim that. Each had a student who was good in history, and in each group, a student who was disruptive. I guess I had two roles in our group. In all, the groups had six students. Instead of being in rows, she had us encircle our deck facing each other in groups.

She set up ground rules. Basically, each group had to turn in assignments for each subject. She would determine what the assignment would be. For each group it would be different. The group had to make sure each person in that group contributed equally to that assignment. The group did not have the option to determine what an equal portion was. That, Ms. Bailey would determine!

LIFESTYLE MANAGEMENT

Of course, as the first few assignments were being turned in, we found out very quickly if someone did not do their fair share of the assignment, because it was not accepted. When the group tried to pick up the slack because somebody in the group did not do their part or was not willing to do the work, the assignments came back with things added to it, thus everyone had to do more. When the assignments came back a second time, the group made sure everyone contributed equally, whether they liked it or not.

I must admit that was a remarkable year. Everyone learned a lot. The classroom was not disruptive, no time was wasted, and learning was fun. Everyone learned and more than just the subject matter. We learned that each have a responsibility to do as much as everyone else and contribute what they can, how they can. No If's, And's or But's! That had to be a gratifying experience to anyone who may have been slow or not such a good student academically, KNOWING that the grade they got was the grade they earned. Because Mrs. Bailey was observant, everyone had to do equal parts before we moved on to the next assignment. So all benefited!

I learned much later in graduate school about group dynamics. Ms. Bailey did all the right things.

* Everyone was unique and different in their traits and skills,
* Focusing attention and energy toward the group,
* There was peer pressure,
* Even coaching by the other students to get everyone up to par,
* When the projects were finished, we all moved on together,
* Plus, the camaraderie that developed through teamwork.

Socially, during this stage, we are starting to change. We initiate separations here, we begin to form our cliques of friends, we are becoming more rigid and start self-imposing limits. Family starts to become a separate unit itself. Still, our needs are being met fairly successfully. If not, it is usually due to our contrariness.

High school stage (thirteen to late teens) In this stage, we are coming into our own socially. We are becoming very opinionated of many things. We tend to form our cliques of friends, and if you're not in that clique by now, you might as well forget it, because you are not going to be unless you do something exceptional or have something the individuals within that clique wants. This is not necessarily a bad thing. Now an individual has to live up to certain expectations. This can be a driving force in one's development. It can be good or bad. Unfortunately for many, the only thing we have to do to get accepted into a particular clique, gang, or group of people is use (chemicals or drugs) or commit an immoral act. This stage puts us in a direct path of choosing negative versus positive activity which we discussed in chapter four. This can be the beginning of enhancing or destroying our character, our uniqueness, and/or our individuality.

Once again, another large chunk of that well-rounded social being has been removed during this stage. Society, beginning with the school system, is becoming more rigid. We are in our pre-specialization stage of our development. The school system expects us to choose a course of study, general studies, college prep, vocational training, or other education alternatives to prepare us for the future.

Our own choice of recreational activity is becoming specialized as we discussed earlier. Now we are hanging out with specific people for specific tasks. For example, the drama club. This group of people gathers for practice, study, or performances. The same goes for sports and other extracurricular activities. Outside of those specific activities, we may not come in contact with those same people for any other reason. Things in our social realm start separating very distinctly. This is where the *satellite social units* start to evolve. We connect with certain people for certain task and purpose. Earlier in life there was an overlapping of activities, and socially, things blended together. For instance, up until this point, we would still bring friends to our homes or include them in some of the family activities. We could include others, friends, and/or family on the spur of the moment for any activity when the opportunity arose. It was all good!

Now, there is no way you are going to do anything with Mom and Dad. Trips to visit Grandma or shopping with Mom aren't going to happen. It has been replaced by being dropped off at the mall. Or

LIFESTYLE MANAGEMENT

worse yet, isolating oneself in your room with a cellphone and/or computer hooked up to the Internet.

We can actually diagram our support systems, as explored in the last chapter, quite distinctly and purposefully into separate social units. Our support system is starting to become very structured. Generally, it is in this stage, where we may start feeling that all of our social needs are not being met. We may even feel like something is missing in our life. Of course, we're growing and starting to experience different emotions and different biological desires, all of which compound the social complexity of each individual.

College stage (late teens to early twenties) In this stage, the real separation of our social support system begins. Here, multiple major changes occur socially. The path of each individual may vary, but socially, the units are very similar. The largest social unit we had in the last stage, where we came in contact with most people consistently, was our school. That may be replaced by a larger school (college or university) where instead of hundreds or maybe a few thousand students, we are in close proximity of several thousand on a daily basis. Our gang/clique is now limited to two or three which are our roommates or special relationships we develop early on in this new environment. There are thousands of people, but we have two or three good buddies, good friends who we go to different social events with, hang out with, and confide in. Our extracurricular activity is now in a one or two highly specialized specific activity areas. In the college environment, you may have one, or two, and occasionally a few more particular separate social units within this large unit. This is the classroom you share with others majoring in the same field of study. If you are there on scholarship or just want to perfect your skill(s), and if you don't perform to expectations, you're eliminated from the group, major, team, fraternity, or sorority, etc. Each separate social unit becomes structured, rigid, and purposeful. Now, there are very distinct separations between all of our social units. These are typical of a large college environment. If you didn't choose that path, the next most common large social environment people may choose in this stage, is the workplace. Another very common one is the military. These are the major three, and tend to be the largest groups

DESOCIALIZATION

(social units) individuals in this age and stage find themselves in. As you can see, each is purposeful and rigid. If you don't respond and perform to the expectations, you won't be there very long. We come in contact with great numbers of people on a daily basis in these social environments, but we are not there to gratify our social needs. We are there to perform specific duties and tasks. We also have our much smaller activity specific groups which we will come in contact with and join for a few hours a day or week, in order to partake in whatever is expected of that group. That is it.

We may find a church, spend an hour or so there once a week, and may not see nor have any other contact with those people until next week. We may see our small group of close friends who we do things with nightly, a few times a week, just on the weekend, or maybe when we are on break, leave, or vacation (if at all). So it goes with all our specialty groups, and limited and separate contacts.

There you have it, *separate social units.* This sets the stage socially for the next stage of our life.

Early productive stage (mid-twenties–) Here, even our largest social environment/unit is limited. For most, this large social unit is the workplace. This work environment is where we spend the majority of our waken day. We are being paid to do specific tasks. We are not there to socialize, yet it is where we come in contact with most people consistently. We may still have our specialized activities in much smaller social units. If we are lucky, we still get together a few times a week to perform whatever activity that unit requires.

We have already discussed, in this stage we tend to stick with the one or two activities we were exceptionally good at during our specialization stage of development. We are now beginning to raise our families, which means our own specific interests may be set aside. Or, at the very least, the pursuit of our own interests is limited due to time we are devoting to the family and work. If you are lucky, you still have a few of your clique of friends that are still in your life. If a few are still around, the time we have to devote to them and that relationship is very limited. There never seems to be enough time in the day to effectively gratify the demands of work, family, and self.

LIFESTYLE MANAGEMENT

I remember when I was in this stage, I was so excited about what I was doing and what I would like to do. I was a few years into my career, shortly after purchasing our first home. I came home from work one day and speaking with my spouse, sharing all my ideas. I spoke to her of all the things I wanted to do and accomplish, at work and home. I remember making a statement, "If only there were forty-eight hours in a day, I could get so much more done."

My spouse stopped what she was doing, squared up with me, and looked me right in the eye. What she said changed my way of thinking for the rest of my life. This is what she said so matter-of-factly, "If there were forty-eight hours a day, you would still be trying to stuff ten pounds of shit into a five-pound bag." I know my eyes opened wide, I stared at her, looked into her beautiful eyes, and realized her words are true. Also thinking, *She actually said that!* She did!

I acknowledged her insight and wisdom from that moment on. I am glad, God in all his wisdom, made the day as it is. I always tell people when it comes to managing our lives, we have twenty-four hours a day. It does not matter who we are, whether you or me, President of United States, or a homeless person on the side of the street. We all have twenty-four hours a day to contend with. It is how we choose to utilize that time by the selection of activities we use to fill our day which will determine how effectively we manage our life.

Yep, I'm glad we only have twenty-four hours in a day. What I get done, I get done. What I don't, I don't. It will be there tomorrow! Maybe it is this which causes me to be so excited, when I wake up in the morning, knowing I have things to get done today. It brings to mind Matthew 6:24–33.

In this stage, our support system is starting to shrink. We may have more social units and satellite units than we ever had before. Examples: church, political groups, civic groups, social clubs, volunteer organizations, etc. Other than work and family, the time devoted to the other social units that are needed and warranted for our own well-being is even more limited.

Late productive stage (late forties to mid-sixties) In this stage, nature and society have taken its course. We still have the largest social unit—our work environment. Still, for many, this being where we spend the majority of our day. Socially, it's not very productive but we have some camaraderie that has developed over the years. Our families have grown and moved away, developing families of their own, thus having little time to spend with us, except when they drop off the grandkids. That is, if they still live locally. If they moved out of state or the country, we may see them a few times over the course of the year.

In this stage, the activities we once enjoyed, we have more than likely let go. Some of them we may have stopped years ago. After doing them for forty years or more of our life, we have become tired of doing them, they no longer interest us. As I mentioned in previous chapters, we stick with activities until we have just worn them out over decades of doing them. If we haven't replaced them with new interests, as many so often don't, then those few social units no longer exist. This fact is what kept me in business for so long.

Have we kept up with our social clubs (women's club, Shriners/Masons, Eastern Star, Moose, Elks, etc.)? What I hear so often is, "I paid my dues annually, but I haven't gone to a meeting in years."

So the benefit of such clubs socially is worthless, but the sense of duty and our willingness to want to help in some way keeps us connected, keeps us paying the dues. (Remember the service component of the basic social needs?)

At this point in our lives, our support systems have shrunk tremendously. We still have our work environment which now becomes even less socially gratifying. This is due to many of our colleagues who may have retired, died, or moved on. The home and family may consist of our spouse and occasional visits from our children or grandchildren. Our social support systems may only be gratifying one or two of the five basic needs sufficiently.

Retirement stage (mid-sixties on) Okay, you may have guessed it, the largest social unit we had for the last forty-plus years no longer exists—our work environment, the place where we came in contact with most people for the majority of our life, despite the limited social benefits. It has been the one constant in our life socially for decades. Now, it's gone through no fault of our own just because we reached a certain age. Our family unit is very small and may consist of just you and your spouse. That is, if you both are still together and weathered the storms, trials and tribulations that the course of a lifetime has presented and blessed you with.

The rare contact we may have with family is probably just major holidays or events (weddings and funerals). Our sons and daughters are too busy, or too old, or set in their ways to travel to come see us. Our grandchildren have started their own families and are in their productive stages and are too busy to visit with us. In the latter reaches of this stage, we may not feel able to even attend our church services. The social unit that is constant may be just you and your spouse.

I refer to this stage as the *Christmas card stage*. We read the obituaries to see who to remove from the list of cards to send. Very few of our social needs are being met; very little of our social support system exists.

Isolation stage. If something happens to your spouse, then you have the final stage of the desocialization process. We are alone when we are in this social stage. None of our social needs are being met.

As you can see, socially, we may experience huge impacts at different stages of our life if we follow the status quo of our societal structure during whatever stage we may be in at any particular time in our life. This is what we can expect, as you may have already noticed and experienced, as you passed through various structured social phases our society herds us into. For many of the stages we may have fond memories. Others you may recognize where damages have occurred in you socially.

This is the typical structure of our society and what it tends to set us up for socially. But we don't have to let this structure limit us. It can, and in many cases, does allow us to develop the social skills we need to function in our society.

Every time I go through this process with a group (whether at a conference or treatment facility), it saddens me. Sad, but true!

This is the course we have or will follow because our society is structured this way Please keep in mind, just because this happens to be the societal structure set up for us, it doesn't mean we have to be set-up by it. In no way, does this have to limit our social development. We can, and many of us do, constantly make adjustments to counteract the effects of this societal course. We can maintain healthy and productive support systems throughout our life, as we change and make adjustments within our lifestyle throughout the course of our life. It does take effort, willingness, as well as insight to be willing to change and modify our support system as we progress through life's changes.

If we don't or are not willing to, we follow this continuum I have just taken you through. We have all seen people who have followed it to a "T" and have found themselves in specific stages at various times in their life. We have seen the effects it has on the individual, friends, family, and neighbors.

Once I reach this phase of the lifestyle management program, I like to have each participant rate themselves on this *desocialization scale*.

By this, I mean, where do you find yourself on this continuum at this time in your life? Keep in mind the five basic social needs. Are you effectively gratifying these?

Intimacy – Are you getting the intimacy you need from the special people in your life?

Recreative – Are your activities rejuvenating you regularly enough to keep you refreshed and vibrant? Does your circle of friends help you gratify your specific interest?

Work – Is your work challenging, paying the bills. Are you comfortable with the people you are working with or for?

Service – Are you benefiting others, with no reward or expectation of personal gain other than helping someone in need?

Spirituality – Are you connecting with others with similar beliefs? Are you accepting and seeking sacred time to devote to your Creator?

Are your social connections fulfilling these basic five social needs or distracting you from them?

Also keep in mind that at any age or stage we happen to be in, at any time in our life, we can feel that we are in any one of the other stages of the desocialization scale as outlined. It mainly depends on whether or not our social needs are being met effectively.

Example, someone age-wise (3-5yrs of age) may fit into the preschool stage, but due to circumstances they are facing in their life, may feel isolated and alone. They may be in the late retirement or isolation stage socially.

On the other hand, someone age-wise (65+yrs of age) may actually be in retirement, now time is not an issue. They may be extremely social and have a great support system, rating them in the high school stage socially.

Are you in the:

Infancy stage: Where all your social needs are being met very effectively with no effort on your part.

Toddler stage: Where all your needs are being met. Life is not necessarily an open book socially any longer. We have some apprehensions. We associate people with certain expectations.

Preschool stage: Where your needs are still being met. Socially, all units still blend together and mix regularly. We start acknowledging differences in people for a variety of reasons—mom, dad, boys, girls, family, friends, strangers. We may actually start recognizing and noticing the differences in race, color, religion. The world may not be as safe a place as we once acknowledged in the previous two stages. Still, our social needs are being met very effectively. The difference in this stage is now you have expectations put upon you socially.

Elementary school stage: Here a big chunk is taken out of our social well-being. We are still getting our needs met very effectively. You have strong social support systems. Life, socially, may still be fairly unstructured; societal-wise structure is initiated.

High school stage: Here is where the separation process starts to take hold. It is an awkward time socially. It is more difficult to connect. We may still have several blended social units. We may or may not be getting our needs met very effectively.

College stage: This stage is where all blended and natural social support ends. All of our interactions are structured, rigid, and purposeful. There are few truly intimate contacts as we enter this stage, though we have lots of contacts for lots of reasons forming more rigid social units.

DESOCIALIZATION

Early productive stage: Here all of our social units are very rigid, structured, and not as socially productive. We are now more focused on earning a living than gratifying our own social needs, thus not meeting them as effectively. In fact, your own social needs may not be met as we focus our energies on work and family.

Late productive stage: Here, very few of our social needs are being met. Maybe some partially.

Retirement stage: Here there is almost no social support system, very few of our social needs are being met.

Isolation stage: Here none of our social needs are being met.

So where did you rate yourself?

Are you in the infancy stage socially where all your social needs are being met without any expectation from you?

Or are you in the toddler stage where you get a lot and don't have to give too much socially?

Or are you in a preschool stage where there is little structure but there are rules to follow, good support system, needs are still met with little effort on your part?

Or are you in an elementary/middle school stage where life has become a little bit more rigid and we start self-inflicting social limitations and have a fair to good support system?

Or are you in a high school stage where life is more structured and awkward with some difficulty connecting, fairly good support system, and some social needs may not be getting met effectively?

Or are you in a college stage where everything you do is rigid, structured, purposeful, and performance-related, your support systems are beginning to shrink, and most needs are being met on a small scale?

Or are you in an early productive stage where you are giving a lot and getting very little in return socially?

Or are you in a late productive stage where very few of your social needs are being met?

Or are you in a retirement stage where you are not giving much and not getting much socially?

Or are you in an isolation stage where you have withdrawn from society or feel that society has abandoned you?

LIFESTYLE MANAGEMENT

It's important to note that throughout our life we may bounce in and out of each of the various social stages. In this chapter, we explored what our society sets us up for as we move, grow, and evolve through the processes of development and the structural phases of our society. It does not mean that no matter what age or societal stage we are presently in at any giving time during our life has to hold true. This representation I have just reviewed with you, can be and is a reference point. It will help us determine the level of productiveness offered from the social support we have or are experiencing, at any given time.

Let me explain. I have worked with many people at various stages of their life who fall within different stages of the societal spectrum. Their present age or phase in the societal structure did not match their own sense or level of support they felt available in their life. Someone who is experiencing psychological difficulties can be constantly around people twenty-four/seven and feel totally alone and isolated. So when rating yourself, rate according to how effectively you feel your needs are being met.

Did you rate yourself accurately?

Are you comfortable with your rating?

My wish for everyone is that we rank ourselves within the first five stages. For it is here where we have very productive social support systems, and the closer we get to the middle stages the more balanced we tend to be. For here, we are not only getting our needs met effectively, we in turn gratify the needs of others.

This is as it should be!

Chapter 12

Communication

As I stated from the beginning of this book, you will be learning more about yourself than you probably ever cared to. These are final notes in closing this self-exploratory journey, and hopefully, a new beginning for many of you.

The stepping stone and key to meeting our needs as well as the needs of others is communication. When it comes to communication, the superficial things in our life are easy to talk about. The important things are those that are truly meaningful and beneficial. Personal things are those that are the most difficult to express due to the very physiological and cognitive processes which can interfere, as outlined and discussed earlier in the examples.

If you reflect on the *fight or flight syndrome* that occurs within, it's a mechanism built into each of us to supply the adrenaline/energy needed for the task at hand. We really no longer have the chance to do either in cases of meeting our social and emotional needs.

Let me explain. If something is not resolved in our life, taking flight is not going to get us any closer to resolution. Actually, it just furthers the distance to the resolution literally and figuratively. Fighting, well, you see the dilemma here!

In this day and age, fighting just drives a bigger wedge into the problem. It can create physical damage, a lawsuit, and greater animosity instead of resolution. Fight or flight—neither sounds like a good option. The fact is, we only have one choice between the two, and that choice is to fight.

But ... here is that word again. The Big butt. The choice weapon for the fight—the only appropriate weapon which will lead to resolution—is communication.

I mean, *real communication* which is all but extinct in this social media-driven society and world we live in today which is more monologue than the dialogue that is needed.

We tend to avoid face-to-face interaction at all costs today. It is easy to see why, because of the reasons explored earlier. We should not expect resolution of any kind without dialogue and sharing of emotions that may accompany it. Without this intimate sharing of emotion, seeing and feeling the expression that is accompanying the communication, it is hard to get the true message. Our ability to connect and empathize, is enhanced when we have all aspects of communication. Without being able to see the conflict one is having while verbalizing and feeling the emotion, it is difficult to understand fully. All are necessary and imperative, when leading us to the most effective response. To be able to see and not only to hear the issue and to feel the conflict, processing it and responding to it effectively is imperative to true understanding.

I just shared with you the four components of communication. No communication is truly complete until all of the following components are met effectively.

1. *Sending a verbal message.* The conveying of information is the first component of any communication.
2. *Receiving the message.* Someone has to receive and listen to the verbal message.
3. *Processing the message.* The information needs to be understood verbally, nonverbally and processed proficiently before someone can respond effectively.
4. *Appropriate response.* The feedback one would expect from the information presented.

COMMUNICATION

Let's look at today's typical means of interaction. Notice I did not say communication. What we have here for the most part is detached interaction.

Examples of social media:

> *Texting:* monologue
> *Email:* monologue
> *TV:* monologue
> *Radio:* monologue
> *Computer:* monologue
> *Phone/cell:* monologue and dialogue, no one answers until the call is screened. When they do answer or return the call, you may hear the emotion, although there is distance and visual detachment.
> *Newspapers:* monologue
> *Magazines:* monologue
> *Cards:* monologue
> *Letters:* monologue (In most cases, people don't respond.)
> *Mail:* monologue

The basic interactive requirements of life are becoming monolistic.

- Shopping: instead of going to the store, order online.
- Food: instead of going to the store, order prepackaged meals with all the ingredients.
- Banking: electronically.
- Interviews: Skype, online, video.
- Selecting a date or mate: online.
- Picking up a date or friend: texting from the driveway.
- Intimate dining: everyone is texting and/or emailing at the table.
- Asking for directions: GPS ("It is easier and more efficient most of the time.")

LIFESTYLE MANAGEMENT

We choose easy; there is less conflict. We have forgotten how to communicate. We don't know how to resolve conflict, internally or externally. So instead of resolution, we create more conflict in an attempt to get some sort of response from others. In many cases, without really even understanding what the true/real conflict may be.

We can all become better communicators and teach others around us to be better communicators, also. I have used a variety of exercises in my treatment sessions and workshops that provoke specific emotions, and require use of one or more of the four components of communication and recognizing them. During this exercise, I will number each component so people in the treatment setting or workshop can easily identify the component by the number. This will generally become the joke of the day. During breaks, you hear participants conversing and say to one another, "You missed number one" or "You must not have completed number three effectively." This will make sense in a moment.

See below:

Component #1 – Sending the message.
Component #2 – Receiving the message.
Component #3 – Processing the message or information.
Component #4 – Appropriate feedback.

During this exercise, I started by saying something to the group or to the individual. I would always prepare a statement so I would correctly present the information. This is the number one component. Depending on the information, I would add some drama into the presentation with appropriate emotion attached to match the message. This also may assist with the components number one and two - presentation and receiving. This is due to more receptive channels being utilized while receiving the information.

Next, we would individually review the responses of the group to the information presented. During the exercise, we would label each component and explore which one they had difficulty with. We knew number one—sending the message—was good; all heard and agreed.

COMMUNICATION

Number two poses problems for many of us. Statistics tell us that the best listeners pick up about thirty percent of verbal information. How many of us consider ourselves to be one of the best listeners? If your answer is, "probably Not," Then that means, more than likely, we will pick up even less.

All the more reason to pay attention to the nonverbal information–the tones, expressions, and the emotions—that goes along with the message.

Number three is processing the information, knowing what we know about our poor listening skills, plus the many distractions we let creep into our lives. If we are picking up at best, thirty percent, and we respond to that thirty percent 100%, the person sending the message is going to feel cheated.

Let me put this into perspective. You need $100. You know I care about you and I am always willing to help. You ask me for $100 and explain why you need it. I reach into my wallet and give you thirty dollars. You're bewildered. You are thinking, *What's this? It is only a third of what I need.* I turn walk away and go about my business, completely content that I helped my friend, and you're feeling cheated. You are wondering what happened to this relationship when, in fact, nothing happened to the relationship. I am still a very caring and concerned partner in this relationship. It was just a breakdown in the processing of the information, which is #3. I am a good listener; my wife doesn't think so. I heard thirty percent, responded 100% to that, so why is my friend thinking I am not concerned about his needs?

It is so important to confirm components number two and three, to make sure they received the information correctly, and understand it. This can be done by simply asking them to repeat what you just said. Then you can confirm whether they got number two effectively. If not, then you can reiterate the information. This will help with processing if there are no other issues going on with the receiver, such as illness, hearing loss, or cognitive deficits.

The sender of the information is always looking for number four—appropriate feedback. But all parties must keep in mind that appropriate feedback is not always what we want to hear, even when it is appropriate.

Let me give an example. Many years ago, when my first child was six or seven years old, she was invited to a sleepover. We knew the people whose children would be attending, we knew the family hosting, and we thought it would be a good idea. My daughter had a wonderful time. We paid for that wonderful time for the next three to four days. Next time my daughter asked to go to a sleepover, I asked her what she would be doing. Her response was, "Daddy we're going to have so much fun. We will stay up all night playing games, watching movies, eating all kinds of goodies, treats, snacks, and pizza." She was so cute!

The response was "No."

No six-year-old needs to be staying up all night long, eating a bunch of junk food, and then being miserable for the next four days. It's not healthy for her or us.

Was the feedback (number four) an appropriate response? Yes!

Was it what she wanted to hear? No!

By reviewing each step of the communication components, it is easy to determine where the breakdown takes place or may have taken place. By confirming each component with the other individual(s), we assist others to be better communicators. By recognizing each component during conversation, we will become better communicators ourselves.

Personally, I have many ideas and see things in great detail. I am at a loss to why others don't see what is so obvious to me. Occasionally, despite my best effort to explain and outline whatever it is that I may be attempting to communicate, the point just does not get across. Plus, maybe my accent can be a factor. Thus I have trouble with number one, so I am doomed from the get-go. Being aware of this, I must set myself up to be clear that the proper message is being sent and absorbed.

We can and should set ourselves up to be better communicators. We will never regret it!

I thoroughly enjoyed taking my two youngest children, my daughter and son, to and from their colleges which were a few hours

COMMUNICATION

away. We were set up for conversation. We were in the vehicle in close proximity with a few hours to discuss any number of things. The driving—a mundane task—offered a slight buffer, if and when needed. The time and environment were set for us to focus on each other's thoughts, ideas, and questions.

I looked forward to those moments. Time would fly by and we both would get glimpses of each other's insights, knowledge, concerns, projects, dreams, and visions. I miss those opportunities to better know and understand those around me.

So start becoming a better communicator right now, today!

If your needs are not being met, there is more than likely a breakdown in one or more of the four components. Start by asking yourself, "Am I sending the information effectively and thoroughly?" If so, look to the second component. Remember, the best listeners pick up about a third of what is being conveyed verbally.

Are you or the people around you some of the best listeners? If your answer is yes, a third of the battle is won.

I am not going to stick my neck out and say I am one of the best listeners. I'll be proven wrong, probably seventy-five percent of the time. I think I am a very good listener. I won't say I am one of the best which means I'm getting less than the thirty percent.

Being the caring, concerned person that I am, I'll respond to the information or request 110%. This, in turn, at the very best, gives the sender forty percent of their request. Thus, needs are only partially met.

To reiterate what I mentioned earlier, one party is content, believing they more than met the request. The other party gets less than half of what is needed and is discontent because their needs are not resolved.

How many times have you said this statement or heard others say it? *"I told them once, I ain't telling them again!"*

Well, if you stick with that philosophy, you had better be satisfied with thirty percent or less of what you need.

Simply by confirming the number two component by asking the receiver to tell you what they heard or understood you to say. Let them process it first, and it will help if you ask them in advance to process what you are about to say before they respond. This will alert the individual to hopefully pay better attention and be more receptive of number one.

This will also prepare them for number three. They know they will be expected to process what is about to be said, which gears the brain to do so. It is kind of an advanced warning system. When numbers one, two, and three take place and are confirmed, we are ready for number four. If the request is not met, the sender can ask for the reasoning of the receiver's conclusion. If an agreement is reached, communication is complete.

Remember, the appropriate feedback (number four) may not meet our request! We still experienced complete communication. Now, the sender must decide to continue to communicate their needs or negotiate. Or come to the realization that their needs are not going to be met here. At this point, they must decide whether or not we need to seek new resource options, where they can get their needs met more productively?

When communication is effective, our messages don't get mixed or misinterpreted. We don't have to keep beating a dead horse, so to speak, and we can get on with our lives. True/real communication resolves conflict. It may not and generally does not change our convictions. It does however without question in those circumstances, after the necessary dialogue has taken place, lets us know whether or not we are barking up the wrong tree.

As with all activity, as referenced in the early chapters of this book, when the activity is completed, the internal message is *it is time to move on!*

Well, you are done with this book.

You know what to do!

So let us do so, and in the process, manage our life as productively as we can.

Conclusion

Lifestyle management is an ever-changing and evolving process. Upon reading this book and completing the exercises, you have the base knowledge. You can start to make more effective choices of your activity involvement. Which can help you create a more productive, balanced, and healthy lifestyle.

Life, and the enjoyment of it, is always a matter of choices. These final notes in the closing of this self-exploratory journey will hopefully be a new beginning for each of you. The beginning of a more healthy and enjoyable existence for all who understand the contents.

Maybe the title of this chapter should be *The Wrap-Up*. Or maybe *The Unwrapping*, which would make more sense and be more to the point? For life is an unfolding, not-so-much of a mystery!

All actions and all events are, or at the very least, can be purposeful. Certainly, every situation within every stage of our life offers unique and different perspectives and opportunities. Throughout life and each phase of it, opportunities and events are not always planned. They just present themselves. Whether it is fate, fortune, misfortune, dumb luck or disastrous, life goes on. We grow, we learn, we experience it. We decide how to react or not to react to what is presented to us.

We control very few things in life, I have found three. Only three! Those are, as mentioned earlier in this book—**our thoughts, our emotions, and our perspectives**, it is these that determine our actions.

With that said and with the knowledge, and I hope understanding, you now have, about the most important person in your life—*you!*

CONCLUSION

You can make the best decisions and follow through with actions to manage your life as productively as possible. When you do and if all align with our purpose, destiny is found. One day, the true reward of this life will be presented to you!

The acknowledgment of a life well lived!

I sincerely hope you enjoyed reading this book. By now you may agree that you have learned more about yourself than you ever expected to. At the very least, you should have a greater understanding of what makes up the uniqueness of each individual. Take this new awareness and have confidence in your knowledge. Love the creature you were created to be! Have faith in yourself and in our Lord God! If not, you can definitely take this to heart and know God does not make mistakes. You are given life—a gift to you! You are the God-given gift to the world! You have been created beautifully and wondrously!

Yes, you are wonderful! That is a given; you don't have to prove it. By your choices in your life, do nothing nor seek anything that will disprove this fact. Throughout our life, we learn from each decision and each experience. May we always seek wisdom.

A quote from Proverbs, "Seek purpose; seek treasures that will not perish."

One day you will know that you lived a life, received the gift, became the gift, and lived the lifestyle for which you were created.

The beginning!

Glossary

Activity. (a) The act of doing work, chores, and play, (b) Have to dos, need to dos, want to dos.
Balance. Reaching equilibrium.
Balance point. A pleasing harmony of various elements; a harmonious existence.
Basic behaviors. Eat, sleep, secrete, mate, play.
Basic social needs. Intimacy, recreation, work, service, spirituality.
Chores. The responsibilities we have to maintain ourselves and our properties.
Components of communication. Send, receive, process, feedback.
Components of self. Physical, intellectual, social, emotional, spiritual.
Excessive exercise. Physical movement that which is beyond the basic requirements of your daily routines.
Leisure. A segment of time; spare time.
Life. A gift; an opportunity given to us by our Creator.
Lifestyle. What we do with the gift of life.
Limiting factors. Things that interfere, limit, or prevent us from doing what we need to do when attempting to achieve a balanced lifestyle.
Play. The act of participating.
Productive lifestyle. Experiencing contentment and peace within ourselves during the course of our life. Gratifying our needs and those of others; pursuing for what we were created.
Recreation. An experience of refreshment of mind and body through diverting activity.
Three major limiting factors. Knowledge, socialization, resources.
Work. Whatever our job is in life depending on our age.

GLOSSARY

Six categories of activity. Creative, intellectual, physical, social, solitary, and spectator.

> *Creative expression.* Activity that allows us to tap into our creative juices; any activity that is unique, new, and different from our ritualistic routines.
> *Intellectual stimulation.* Activity that stimulates the mind.
> *Physical exercise.* Activity requiring movement.
> *Social interaction.* Activity involving others.
> *Solitary relaxation.* Activity only involving oneself.
> *Spectator Appreciation.* Activity involving any or all our senses.

Self Exploratory Exercises

Balanced Lifestyle Survey

There are six activity classifications / involvement areas that will assist you in developing a balanced lifestyle. These are Creative Expression, Intellectual Stimulation, Physical Exercise, Social Interaction, Solitary Relaxation and Spectator Appreciation. Everyone needs all of these to some degree. Frequently these are met in ways we do not realize. It is important to remember that different people fulfill different needs Through their activity(s)pursuit. These listed represent but a very small fraction of things one can do to oblige their needs for a well-balanced lifestyle. These activities cover a wide range of activities classified within their specific whelm. It should be pointed out that this test is intended to provide a stimulant to look into one's own strong and weak involvement areas. Here is how you should score. Place a "check" in the appropriate column. Score 3-points for "frequently", 2-pionts for "occasionally" and 1-point for each "never". Add up each section, a score of 18-23 is considered normal for the individual sections.

LIFESTYLE MANAGEMENT

SOCIAL INTERACTION

	Frequently	Occasionally	Never
I invite Friends to my home			
I seek / make new friends			
I write letters / sending greeting cards			
I attend parties / family gatherings /social events			
I play cards or other board games			
I visit my neighbors			
I attend club, civic meetings / church			
I go to community events			
I argue, debate			
I make social phone calls			

CREATIVE EXPRESSION

I cook			
I plan parties / special events			
I draft/ draw project plans			
I do handicrafts, woodworking, mechanics			
I write poetry, stories or songs			
I play an instrument (S)			
I paint, draw pictures or projects			
I plan or do home redecorating			
I participate in the performing arts (music, drama, dance)			
I doodle or sketch			

BALANCED LIFESTYLE SURVEY

PHYSICAL EXERCISE

	Freq'y	Occa'y	Never
I work in the garden or yard			
I take walks / hikes			
I avoid taking the elevator			
I take part in active sports (bowling, swimming, golf etc.)			
I dance			
I ride a bicycle / exercise cycle (fitness apparatus)			
I refinish furniture or antiques			
I fish, hunt or camp / outdoor activities			
I pick wild flowers / plants			
I wash / detail the car			

SPECTATOR APPRECIATION

I watch television			
I go to movies			
I watch children at play			
I watch birds and animals			
I go to ball games or other sports events			
I travel or go sightseeing			
I people watch			
I go to the theatre, stage plays			
I attend concerts			
I notice changes in buildings and landscapes			

LIFESTYLE MANAGEMENT

INTELLECTUAL STIMULATION	Freq'y	Occa'y	Never
I attend lectures /church / school			
I visit the museums / attend cultural events			
I discuss controversial subjects			
I go to the library			
I actively participate in service to others (volunteer, help others)			
I collect something (s)			
I read			
I keep up with current events			
I look at travel sights, guides, brochures			
I take time to answer questions			

SOLITARY RELAXATION

I pray or mediate			
I work crossword or other puzzles			
I hum, sing or whistle			
I listen to music			
I keep a scrap book, photo album, diary			
I sit by myself			
I loaf, relax, do nothing			
I day dream			
I watch the snow fall or listen to the rain			
I take naps			

Group Benefit Exercise!

To complete this exercise and identify your major motivators review the list below numbers 1 through 10. You have nine sections; each section compares one activity benefits against another. Compare each then Circle your preference. Example if you prefer #1-relaxation over #2-enjoyment you would circle the 1 if you preferred #6- being helpful over #4-sense of accomplishment you would circle the 6. Note: the numbers in each column 1 – 10 correspond represent the designated benefit they are numbered.

(You may want to review chapter 8 pages 123-124 and 138-142)

1- Relaxation

2- Enjoyment

3- Fitness

4- Sense of Accomplishment

5- Socialization

6- Being Helpful

7- Filling Time

8- Excitement

9- Freedom

10- Creativity

LIFESTYLE MANAGEMENT

1 - 2								
1 - 3	2 - 3							
1 - 4	2 - 4	3 - 4						
1 - 5	2 - 5	3 - 5	4 - 5					
1 - 6	2 - 6	3 - 6	4 - 6	5 - 6				
1 - 7	2 - 7	3 - 7	4 - 7	5 - 7	6 - 7			
1 - 8	2 - 8	3 - 8	4 - 8	5 - 8	6 - 8	7 - 8		
1 - 9	2 - 9	3 - 9	4 - 9	5 - 9	6 - 9	7 - 9	8 - 9	
1 - 10	2 - 10	3 - 10	4 - 10	5 - 10	6 - 10	7 - 10	8 - 10	9 - 10

Totals

1_____   **Top 3 Responses:**

2_____   #1_____ (highest score)

3_____   #2_____ (second highest score)

4_____   #3_____ (third " ")

5_____   [If a tie, find the column you compare both,

6_____   the one you choose ranks first.]

7_____   **Lowest 3 Responses:**

8_____   #1_____ (lowest score)

9_____   #2_____ (second lowest score)

10_____   #3_____ (third " ")

[If a tie, find the column you compare both
the one you did not choose ranks first.]

About the Author

The author grew up in a large family of limited means in Haverhill, Massachusetts, although never lacking in any of the necessities of life. Being the youngest gives one an opportunity to live and observe many of the natural and not so natural aspects of life. Acknowledging the roles of the firstborn, middle children, and the youngest (the author), one sees the course of growth and development. You see the changes and evolution of these life changes socially, emotionally, physically, intellectually, and spiritually.

You know what is coming down the pike!

The youngest, not having much say on things, learns to observe, process, and with some luck, learn from those going before him or her.

The bottom of the pecking order is always on notice. The author guesses there are some perks being the last and least of which he is still trying to figure out what they are.

What he knows he learned is love, selflessness, duty, honor, and respect for self and others. At a young and crucial age, he was given a vision that would change how he would look at and see things for the rest of his life.

The author is married and has three adult children. He was an athlete in high school and at collegiate and amateur levels, participating in football, track and field, and wrestling.

As a Certified Recreation Therapist, he has over forty years of experience assisting people from all walks of life, including the mentally ill, physically challenged, chemically dependent, and those managing pain.

He has strong faith!

He has conducted numerous presentations and workshops covering many aspects of the therapeutic recreation discipline and lifestyle management practice.